FINDING
PEACE

GOD'S PROMISE OF A LIFE FREE
FROM REGRET, ANXIETY, AND FEAR

CHARLES STANLEY

OLIVER
NELSON
™

THOMAS NELSON PUBLISHERS®
Nashville

A Division of Thomas Nelson, Inc.
www.ThomasNelson.com

Published in Nashville, Tennessee, by Thomas Nelson, Inc.

All Scripture quotations are taken from THE NEW KING JAMES VERSION®. Copyright © 1979, 1980,1982 by Thomas Nelson, Inc. Used by permission. All rights reserved.

Library of Congress Cataloging-in-Publication Data

Stanley, Charles F.
    Finding peace : God's promise of a life free from regret, anxiety, and fear / by Charles F. Stanley.
    . p. cm.
    ISBN 0-7852-7297-6
    1. Emotions—Religious aspects—Christianity. 2. Peace—Religious aspects—Christianity. I. Title.
    BV4597.3.S74 2003
    248.8'6—dc21

2003010035

Printed in the United States of America

03 04 05 06 BVG 5 4

This book is dedicated to my two godly children,
Andy and Becky,
whose unconditional love and encouragement have been a
source of strength, joy, and contentment
to their father.

CONTENTS

ONE

WHO'S IN CONTROL?

"Dr. Stanley, I can't rent you a car."

I understood the words the woman across the counter was saying to me, but I could hardly take in the full meaning of her statement.

"You can't?" I asked. "Why not?"

"I don't have a car to rent to you."

A sad fact emerged over the next few minutes. There was *no* car that *any* automobile rental agency could rent to me at that airport. I had planned this trip for weeks, getting everything in place—or so I thought. I had eagerly anticipated this time alone with God in the Great Northwest, photographing places of wonderful natural beauty. I had everything in order—except a car.

I took a cab to the hotel where thankfully, I had a reservation, and went directly to the hotel's restaurant to eat a bite and collect my thoughts. Staring at the pouring rain outside the restaurant's windows, I silently prayed *God, You're in charge.* He knew I didn't want to turn around and fly home. I felt very strongly that the Lord had given His full blessing to my taking this trip—I had been very much at peace as I had mapped out various routes and locations. Once again I reflected, *God, You're in charge.* I had no idea what to do, but I knew that *God* knew. I felt totally dependent on Him.

While I was sitting there, a couple of men came by, and one recognized me. They stopped to introduce themselves and talk for a while. One of them asked me what I was doing in Oregon, and I told them the story of what had happened. He quickly responded, "Don't worry about that! We have three cars, and I'd be happy for you to use one of them. It's in good shape. I'll have a car over here for you in forty-five minutes."

As promised, in less than an hour, the car was at the hotel— and it was a very nice car. I was blessed by this man's spontaneous generosity, I knew that God had sent him directly to me. I was thankful to him and even more grateful to God.

I had a fantastic time photographing there for a couple of days. At the end of the second day, I had the idea to set up my camera in plenty of time to get a good sunset shot from one particular spot along the Oregon coast. When I arrived at that location, which was fairly remote, I unloaded my photographic equipment. While I was standing by my car, I was approached by an elderly woman who recognized me, and we talked for a few moments. Then I transported my gear on foot to the particular vantage point I had selected. I took several photographs as the sun was setting, and then packed everything and started back to the car.

As I reached into my pocket for the car keys, I made a startling discovery . . . no keys. I looked through my bags of camera equipment . . . no keys. I thought, *Did I lean over and drop those keys from my pocket while I was talking to that lady?* I looked carefully around the outside of the car . . . no keys. By this time, the sun was setting and it was starting to get dark. No one else was around. But for the first time, I noticed a fairly large sign at the edge of the parking lot that read, "Warning! Unsafe area. Do not remain here after dark."

Great! I thought. *I'm alone. It's getting dark. And now I learn I'm in an unsafe area.* It was at that moment I saw my keys dangling from the ignition inside the locked car. My heart momentarily sank and I thought, *What a mistake to leave the keys in the car!*

I prayed, "God, You know my location. You know the situation. You know what that sign says. You see my keys. You see *me*. I know You are 100 percent in charge of my life. I don't know what You are going to do, but I'm trusting You to help me."

I felt impressed to walk around the car and try all the door handles, which I had already done. This time, as I pulled on the back passenger-side door latch, to my great amazement it opened. All the other doors were locked tighter than a drum. But that one door opened. I retrieved the car keys, threw my equipment into the car, and drove back to my hotel, praising God all the way!

Two more great days of scenic beauty and photography passed and I found myself following a road next to a river that had a number of waterfalls. It was just about dawn as I entered this beautiful area, but the light wasn't exactly what I had envisioned. I checked my map and saw that Mount Hood was in that immediate area. It couldn't be seen from where I was along the river, but I had a hunch that if I would just follow a back road in a particular direction, I'd come to an area that would give me an open line of sight to the mountain.

Finally I rounded a bend and there it was, Mount Hood, with a field and trees in the foreground. Absolutely beautiful! I continued along the road, hoping for a small body of water that reflected the mountain. To my delight, a small lake soon appeared. I took several photographs, and then I got back in the car, intending to retrace my route, when I happened to notice the gas gauge. This was the first time that day I had looked at it. Unfortunately it was on empty.

I thought back over the route that I had taken to get to that point and realized that I hadn't seen a gas station all morning. For that matter, I had no idea even where I was! I had just been following the roads as I came to them, looking upward and ahead to try to spot the mountain and find a lake.

Again I prayed, "Dear Lord, You are in control." I was keenly aware that for the third time that week, I was in a desperate situation and only God could help me out of it!

About that time a big power-company truck drove up near where I was parked. The man got out, climbed up a pole, adjusted something there, and then came back down. I was waiting for him at the bottom of the pole. I said, "Sir, could you tell me where I might find a gas station?"

He said, "Go up this road about a quarter of a mile, turn left, and it's right there."

I had just enough gasoline to get there.

Had that power-company employee not stopped next to my car, my natural instinct would have been to go back down the roads I had been on, not to go farther down a road that seemed to lead to even greater isolation. I knew that once again God had provided for me in a unique way. Indeed, He was in control!

It seemed every time I turned around that week, I found

myself in a position of begging God for mercy: "Here I am again, Lord. I need You. I belong to You. You are in control of my life. I'm trusting You."

That afternoon I returned to the river, and this time the light was perfect. I got some wonderful shots of those waterfalls. I realized that if I hadn't taken a slight "detour" that morning, I not only would have missed out on seeing the beauty of Mount Hood from a remote location, but I would have missed out on a major miracle of God's protection and provision. Those shots of the waterfalls were a reassurance from God—"See, I'm in control of all your steps, both the ones that seem to be filled with stress and the ones that are filled with pure peace and joy."

As I reflected on that experience, I realized that during that week I was never once afraid, anxious, or worried. I was a little upset with myself for not arranging for a rental car, for locking my keys in the car, and for not paying attention to the gas gauge. Given those mistakes, I was concerned about what I should do or not do, but each time I got into difficulty, I really wasn't afraid, anxious, or worried. Rather, I was aware that I had a big need that I couldn't solve on my own. I had to rely on the One who could solve the problems for me.

A GOD BIGGER THAN OUR CHALLENGES

Long ago I came to the total assurance that God loves me, God knows where I am every second of every day, and God is bigger than any problem life's circumstances can throw at me. I have complete confidence that God is able to take care of any situation and provide an answer to any question or problem—He has all the resources of the universe to draw upon in helping each one of us through any type of crisis if we will trust Him.

Based upon many challenging events in my life, I *know* with deep certainty that God is *always* in control. He will never leave me, turn His back on me, reject me, or withdraw His love from me. He delights in showing me again and again that He is the source of my strength, my provision, my protection, and my ultimate success in life. I have absolutely no doubt that God is in control of every second of my future.

Let me ask you today: Who's in control of *your* life?

> **Because God is in control of your life, and you have a strong, unshakable conviction on this matter, then and only then will you have the necessary foundation to experience what the Scriptures call "the peace that passes understanding."**

Why do I ask? Because it is the crucial question anyone who is seeking peace must ask if they are to find what their hearts so desperately desire. Because God is in control of your life, and you have a strong, unshakable conviction on this matter, then and only then will you have the necessary foundation to experience what the Scriptures call "the peace that passes understanding."

Stop to think about it for a moment, The issue of control is so important in our lives:

If you are controlled by the particular situation you are facing, you can't have peace, because at any second that situation can spin out of control. Life's circumstances can change in a heartbeat.

If some evil power is in control, you're certainly in trouble.

If another person controls you or the circumstance in which

you are involved, you may have peace for a while, but eventually that person may disappoint you and let you down in some way, and you can lose your peace.

If you are in control, you may appear to have the power to guarantee yourself a peaceful existence, but eventually you are going to make a mistake or something/someone will enter the picture to rearrange your circumstances, and before you know it, boom! Trouble with a capital *T* is at your door, and then you will find that your ability to create and control your own serenity was a mere illusion.

But what if God is in control of your life? With Him steering the ship, there's every reason to hope, every reason to feel confident, and every reason to move forward boldly in your life, expecting the best out of every experience.

Some people might ask, "How can God expect me to have peace in my heart when everywhere I turn I'm faced with greed, corruption, anger, terrorist threats, and other forms of evil?" Is it really possible to live in a society such as ours and have genuine peace in our hearts?

The need to answer that question has led me to write this book. Everywhere I turn, in a variety of ways and often with pent-up emotions, people express their need for peace, and they are unable to find it in the midst of a society that seems destined to self-destruct. There is an answer for you, friend. That answer has been so very well expressed in the words of a hymn written by a man who knew God was in control of all things. He found God's peace even in the tragic loss he experienced when his wife and daughters were drowned when their ship sank in the midst of a terrible storm. He wrote:

When peace like a river attendeth my way,
When sorrows like sea-billows roll;
Whatever my lot, Thou hast taught me to say,
"It is well, it is well with my soul."
    (HORATIO G. SPAFFORD, "It Is Well with My Soul")

In my experience and in the lives of thousands, yes, thousands of people who have crossed my path, that is the way life can be—peace in the midst of the storm. Let us look deeper to discover how to find this peace.

TWO

THE FOUNDATION FOR ALL PEACE

S ome time ago, prior to a speaking event, a staff member and I were having a meal in a restaurant on the West Coast. The young woman who was waiting on us appeared to be in her twenties. During the meal, while she was tending our table, I asked her, "If you could ask God for anything in your life, what would you ask Him to do for you?"

Without any hesitation she said, "I'd ask for peace."

A big tear began to make its way down her cheek as she began to tell us about the death of her beloved grandmother just a few days before.

As she shared her story, I learned that nobody in her family believed in God and neither did she. She had not consciously rejected God—she had never really heard about Him. All she knew was that there was a deep restlessness inside, but she had no understanding about how to resolve that inner turmoil, or even what lay at the root of it. Like many people, she was just living from day to day, not having much purpose or meaning in her life.

This woman represents so many in our society today—going through the motions, making ends meet, seeking a way where there seems to be no path for them, pushing on through the obstacles and trying to make sense out of it all.

Many women go through the teen years with a strong motivation to find that "special" man—a prince charming—who will, through marriage, fulfill their dreams and bring an end to the emptiness they may have felt for so long. Most of us know, however, that rarely do partners in a marriage find their spouse able to provide even a small amount of comfort and satisfaction.

Conversely, so many young men grow up seeking to be successful in life—whatever that means! They give life their best effort only to eventually find themselves falling short and struggling to hold on to anything for support and stability. The degrees they earn and the money they make never seem to be enough. So often, they end up feeling inadequate, the dreams they nurtured in their adolescence seem to flitter away, and eventually reality strikes—a reality that brings into question the meaning and purpose of life for them and, if truth were told, for all of us.

Too often, unfortunately, there seems to be no adequate answers to our human dilemma—especially to the question of why we feel so empty and void. Furthermore, there appears to be no satisfactory reason for us to keep putting out our best efforts and still suffering with life's adversities.

The young waitress serving us in the restaurant explained the issue in her terms by saying, "I need peace." Others would say, "I am so lonely." Some would say, "If my spouse would only love me as he/she should, then I would be happy." Different variations but all the same melody: "There is something wrong; I am not happy. I have no peace. What is wrong with me?"

Most who are victims of the messages of our secular society experience this void and do not equate their problem with God. Constantly we are bombarded with their claims. It usually begins with this proposition: "If only you . . ." "If only you were thinner, dressed with more style, drove a Jaguar, lived in a better part of town, made more money . . ."The list goes on and on. None of the above-mentioned highly-prized answers to our problem or any of the hundreds of others offered to us can permanently and satisfactorily provide what we desperately crave.

The young waitress had it right—Most of us feel strongly that we need something more, and the all-encompassing word that so well describes it is, *peace.*

Now, dear reader, as a pastor for more than four decades, I will take the liberty of doing what ministers so often do from the pulpit? I want to be very clear and state emphatically to you that until you have peace with God, you will never experience true peace in this life. This is the most foundational principle in the Scriptures.

THE GOD OF PEACE DESIRES A RELATIONSHIP WITH YOU!

The God who controls all things, who is present in your life, whether you acknowledge Him or not, is the God of Peace. That is His name—Jehovah Shalom, the God of Peace, and He has done a marvelous thing in creating this world and all the elements in it. He has purposely designed it with a plan in mind. And that plan includes *you!*

> **The God who controls all things, who is present in your life, whether you acknowledge Him or not, is the God of Peace.**

Therein lies the problem. If you are unaware that there is a plan or that you are part of that plan, then you will be unable to recognize His signposts along the way. What so many sense as their "loneliness" and others as a "deep void" or "purposelessness" is, in actuality, one of the signals that God has placed within us. It is His programmed message that we need Him. The designer is telling His creation, "Without Me you will never feel complete. I am the only One who can satisfy your deep-seated longings. I will be the source of your peace."

His plan was to create mankind so that we would have a relationship with Him. This relationship would be characterized by love: God's loving us and our loving Him. And through His loving presence, He would protect and provide for us. This idea was and is unique to Judeo-Christian religious thought.

No matter what other relationships we share, what our status is in life, where we have been and what we have done on our life journeys, God designed us to have this intimate relationship with Himself. He knew that out of this intimacy of relationship we could receive His gift to all who follow Him—a deep, lasting, abiding peace that only He can provide to the human heart.

For some of you, however, there is a fundamental problem with this plan. You may never have heard about it, or perhaps you may never have had someone explain it to you in a clear way. Then again, you may have rejected the plan in earlier years for whatever reason, and you now sense deep inside the ongoing emptiness. You know *now* is the time for you to find the answer to your need.

As a youth, I needed a friend to explain the plan to me. I am so grateful it was made clear to me. Basically, I was told that God created the world through His unprecedented power and authority. He created humans and allowed us to enjoy His beautiful world. But our ancestors made wrong choices, and we have continued to do the same ever since. Just like men and women down through the centuries, we have rebelled against His principles and laws. In other words, we sin.

SIN'S DESTRUCTIVE POWER

What happens when we sin? We become self-centered and drift farther and farther away from God and His plan. We gradually reject the idea that we need His presence in our lives, and we begin to follow after our selfish desires rather than listening to the voice of our heavenly Father.

When we are faced with pain, suffering, loneliness, estrangement, and death, we are unable to cope. Why? We don't have the inner resources to bring peace to our troubled hearts. Our souls have become bankrupt. In essence, God made us to fly like eagles, but instead we have become earthbound, miserable creatures who have lost the instincts to be who our heavenly Father created us to be. We find ourselves hopping around, vainly trying to find purpose and meaning in life because we have lost touch with our Creator. His desire is to bring us back into right relationship with Him. Isn't that the desire of your heart?

> **God made us to fly like eagles, but instead we have become earthbound, miserable creatures who have lost the instincts to be who our heavenly Father created us to be.**

This dilemma we face is actually a very good thing because it opens a window to our souls, a window that our loving Father can use to make contact with us again. So many fellow travelers on life's journey live with their souls closed to the possibility that God could or may even want to intervene in their affairs. Just like the young waitress, they have not chosen deliberately to run away from God and to opt for a life of struggles and turmoil. Rather, they simply do not know the path to peace.

Thinking about the path to peace, I have never met a person who woke up one morning and said, "I think I'd like to live in turmoil. I think I'd like to have the whole world around me collapse. I think I'd like to have the rug pulled out from under me today." No! Though there are a few persons I know who seem to enjoy living in the middle of disorder and chaos, most of us don't seek that kind of life. We do not *seek* turmoil. At one time or another, I'm sure most of us have heard someone say, "Oh, for a moment's peace." But surely, the cry of all our hearts is not for just a moment but for a lifetime of peace!

So often, however, turmoil seems to find us. Let me give you a personal example. Not long ago, I was riding a horse while on a photographic excursion high in the mountains. Suddenly my horse began to rear back as if he were going to throw me. Now this particular horse was very mild mannered and surefooted, not at all skittish or high-spirited. I immediately pulled him back a few feet, but again he began to be agitated.

I looked at the path ahead of us and saw no snake, no wild animal, and no obvious danger. I backed up the horse until we were almost wedged between two trees. When I dismounted for a closer look, I saw the problem.

The horse had stepped onto a large nest of wasps, and they had begun to sting him! I immediately turned and ran the opposite direction, and in a few seconds, I heard my horse panting right over my shoulder. He was running away too, following right behind me!

Now, did I intend to lead my horse into the nest? No.

Was I putting my horse to a test of some kind? No.

Was I in a constant state of fear thinking about possible dangers that might confront me on the path we were traveling? No!

Did any of that make any difference once that horse stepped on that large wasps' nest? Not one bit of difference. He got scared, I got scared, and we got out of there as fast as possible!

Those angry wasps stung and swirled without any regard to my lack of intent in disturbing them. And the consequences for both the horse and me were just as real—and in the case of my horse, just as painful—as if I had planned and schemed to create that situation.

Life is like that. Bad things happen. Trouble appears at the most inopportune times. Disaster strikes. And we are left to face the consequences.

In my experience that's the way it is with so many people. We step blindly into a wasps' nest of trouble and find ourselves nursing painful wounds, trying to pull out the stingers and vowing never again to get hurt, only to find that we don't have the power to keep free from the dangers that cross our paths.

But often, sudden tragedy or personal loss can open us up to our need for help, comfort, and guidance. And it is at this very point of need that our kind and loving God can open the window to our hearts. When we give the okay, God will come to our rescue. He does this by helping us understand His plan.

He will teach us about His Son, Jesus, who came into our world to live and die as one of us. He was both God and man at the same time—an amazing truth. You will learn that as a sinless man, Jesus was killed because the religious leaders of His day were threatened because He claimed to be the Savior of the world.

After His death, however, He did something that no one else has ever done—He became alive by the power of God. When He did this, He triumphed over that eventual reality we all must face—death. Jesus then returned to heaven to be with His Father, and He promised all His followers that His presence would remain with them and His peace would never leave them.

There is one caveat: None of us are good enough to make it to heaven by our own efforts. Why would Jesus have had to endure death and suffering if we could do it alone? So, God's plan is for all of us, in every generation and in every nation, to ask for His mercy, confess our sins, and trust Him for our salvation. That's the essence of God's plan for you and me, friend. It is also the fundamental requirement for us to experience God's wonderful, continuous gift of peace.

In summary then, Jesus is the foundation stone of our peace. He bridges the gap between God and man. The Scriptures say, "He is our peace." And what wonderful benefits are ours: forgiveness (no more shame or guilt because of the past), the continuous assurance of God's presence in our lives, and more to the point of this book, *His peace*—the gift that is given to those who begin to follow the Master.

∞

THREE

THE QUALITY OF PEACE GOD GIVES

If you are a student of the Bible or even a casual reader, I am sure you have noticed that God's perspective is often given in the form of comparison and contrast. For example, He often contrasted the rich and the poor—how much easier it is for the poor to get into the kingdom of God than the rich. The Scriptures point out that the wealthy often have a tendency to rely on their notoriety, fortune, status, and associations to help them get into the kingdom; whereas the poor, having none of the above, simply must rely on God's mercy for their way into heaven.

Other examples are those contrasting friends and enemies, wise and foolish persons, darkness and light, and with respect to our topic, the peace that comes from God as opposed to the peace found in this world. Jesus said, "My peace I give to you; not as the world gives . . ." (John 14:27).

Clearly, the Master was stating the peace He gave to His followers was different from that which they could find in the world. When Jesus referred to "the world," He was speaking of the society and culture in which we humans live.

Have you ever been on a troubled sea? I have experienced storms at sea on several occasions and frankly, I have no desire to repeat such experiences! On the surface, the winds can sweep across the ocean at forty, sixty, eighty, one hundred miles an hour, with blowing rain, lightning, thunder, and an overpowering darkness. Waves can rise to twenty, thirty, forty, fifty feet high. A ship in such a storm can be tossed about like a little toy boat. It's easy for an oceangoing craft to be lost in such storms, but underneath the surface, just a hundred feet down, there is no storm; all is perfectly quiet. No sound. No tumult. Not even a ripple of turmoil.

This remarkable fact makes me think about God's peace. It gives me an inkling of what our Lord must have been talking about when He promised His disciples His peace. He told them that because they were His followers, they would have trouble in this world. In fact, He claimed that some of them would be persecuted because they were His disciples. But in spite of this, the promise was made by Him that He would never leave those who followed Him, and His constant presence would be the means whereby they could experience His peace. Do you see the connection between His presence and His peace?

I know a man who some forty-five years ago in his youth was just like the waitress I met on the West Coast—he was active, working hard, and also taking time for some leisure—but in describing his life he said to me, "I was profoundly lonely." He told me that he tried everything to find an answer for the ache inside himself. Until one day, a friend talked to him about Jesus, and God had mercy on him. The window to his soul was opened and he responded to God.

He told me that on that day, the loneliness disappeared and he has experienced a continuous peace. He emphasized that this peace has been present in his life no matter where he has been or what circumstance he has faced—God's abiding, deep, incomprehensible peace has never left him.

THE WORLD'S PEACE OR GOD'S PEACE?

What is the peace offered to us by the world? Some people seem to think that peace, contentment, and happiness are interchangeable terms. For example, I know a number of young people who come from wealthy homes and at a young age go off to the finest college their parents' money can afford. They have plenty of spending money, which invariably seems to end up being spent on alcohol and drugs. They find they can attract people who are more than willing to indulge with them and, as is often the case, indulge in sexual immorality.

After they graduate from college—an experience from which they learned very little practical information and acquired even less wisdom—their parents set them up in well-paying jobs in the "family business." They can afford to live in beautiful homes or condos. By the time these young people turn twenty-five, they are jaded. They have seen it all.

Over the course of these years, I am sure some of them would have said they were happy, perhaps contented, but I don't think you would have heard them characterize their own personal journeys as being peace filled. On the contrary, so often I sense in today's generation almost a spirit of despair—they seek money, clothing, sex, and advancement at any cost. But deep inside they are frustrated by an internal dissatisfaction, never understanding the true source of their emptiness.

Sometimes when I am out of town staying in a hotel, I walk through the bar on my way to the dining room just to see who is there and try to get a sense of why they are there. I am always amazed—the sign at the entrance to the bar may say "Happy Hour," but I see very little happiness on the faces of the people inside. They look stressed-out, weary, lonely, and eager for just about anybody to talk to.

If you would ask one of those people in the bar, "What is it that will make you happy?" you might be surprised at the answer you get. A person said to me not long ago, "If I just had a relationship with someone I really loved and that person loved me, I'd be happy. I'd have peace and joy in my life."

I said, "I agree with you that happiness, peace, and joy lie in a relationship. But not a relationship with another person—a relationship with God!"

To one person an opportunity to go shopping at a huge mall in a big city with lots of money to spend might sound like a recipe for happiness. To another person that might sound like the worst way to spend a day!

To one person, walking alone along a wilderness trail high in the mountains might be a very "happy" way to spend a few hours. To another person such an experience might be one that seems fearful, difficult, or a terrible burden.

Happiness and contentment lie totally within a person's own perceptions and emotions. Nobody and no thing can make another person happy or contented. Happiness and contentment are states of mind that arise out of our perception of people, circumstances, and how they interrelate with us.

Christians believe that ultimately, whether one focuses on being happy, contented, or living a life of peace, the source of these gifts is God. Can you see, however, that these gifts (and they *are* gifts) are different entities? They are not the same. Even the most happy and contented person, over the course of his or her life, often grudgingly admits that something is missing. The humble follower of Jesus knows that the essential ingredient for all persons to be happy, contented, and at peace within themselves is the presence of God.

Remember, what the world offers as "peace" is ultimately an illusion, even though it may appear very concrete. It is like a mirage in the desert. A mirage looks like a body of water. But in fact, it does not exist and therefore is never attainable. A mirage has absolutely no ability to quench thirst.

Remember, what the world offers as "peace" is ultimately an illusion, even though it appears very concrete. It is like a mirage in the desert.

The world regards peace as being the by-product of doing the right deeds, saying the right words, working in the right job, or having the right intentions.

These aren't at all the criteria for peace described in God's Word. Peace is an inner quality that flows out of a right relationship with God. What are the benefits of this peace?

FOUR GREAT CLEAR SIGNS OF GOD'S PEACE

1. GOD'S PEACE TRANSCENDS CIRCUMSTANCES

God's peace is not a denial of reality. God never intends for us to turn a blind eye to the reality of any situation, including evil. Rather, He intends for us to confront reality with our faith and with an abiding peace in our hearts.

Neither is God's peace an escape from reality. We are not transfixed or somehow mentally "removed" from feeling pain or struggling. Peace is not a stupor that dulls our senses. It is not an elimination of responsibility for addressing hard issues and difficult circumstances. Rather, peace is an undergirding rock-solid foundation so that no matter the tears we cry or the sorrow we feel, deep down inside we know with an abiding assurance that God is with us. God is in control, and the joy of the Lord is going to emerge far greater than any depth of agony we may be experiencing.

Part of the reason God allows us to experience sorrow and trials in this life is so we might learn that God has power to sustain us and provide for us all things that produce earthly blessings and eternal benefits.

God's peace has "keeping" or sustaining power in the midst of reality. In her recent book, *Let's Roll,* Lisa Beamer tells of God's sustaining power and His all-encompassing peace as she has walked through the devastating loss of her husband and the other courageous men and women on flight 93 that crashed into the fields of Pennsylvania on September 11, 2001.

All of God's children go through storms in their journeys through life. It is precisely in the "going-through" stage of any crisis that God's peace is most clearly manifested to all.

In one of the most trying times of my life, God gave me such an outpouring of His peace that I was utterly amazed at how calm I felt. It was during a major crisis at our church some years ago. I was able to walk out before thousands of people, knowing in my mind that nearly half of them were "against me," and feel such a calm confidence in my heart that it really didn't matter what any person said or did in that hour. I knew without a shadow of doubt that God was with me and in me, sustaining me on a cushion of His presence and peace. I walked away from that experience saying to the Lord, "I can hardly comprehend that I'm not upset. It is a miracle that I feel so calm inside!"

As I reflected on that particular experience later, I realized that the reason I could be so calm was that I *believed* God's power in me was greater than any power that might come against God's plan and purpose for my life. A favorite Scripture passage for me is, "He who is in you is greater than he who is in the world" (1 John 4:4).

Often, peace is more readily seen and felt in the midst of trial and trouble. I don't know what you may be going through today. You may be grieving the death of a loved one. You may be mourning the loss of a relationship with someone you hold dear. You may be going through a divorce or a time of separation in your marriage. You may be experiencing a severe illness or recovering from a terrible injury. You may have lost a job. You may have lost your life's savings or seen your investments fail. You may be going through pain you never thought you could survive. You may be going through hurt or rejection you never thought you could endure.

Regardless of what you are experiencing, please know this: God is your peace. Put your faith in Him.

2. GOD'S PEACE SURPASSES UNDERSTANDING

Toward the end of his life, the apostle Paul—a man God used to write most of the letters that form the New Testament—wrote a letter to his friends in the city of Philippi. Paul was in prison, and yet he wrote to them: "The peace of God, which surpasses all understanding, will guard your hearts and minds . . ." (Phil. 4:7).

In other words, the peace God gives is something you can't necessarily figure out. You can't always understand how it operates in you. God doesn't intend it to be understood by the human mind or explained in a natural manner. The fact that Paul was chained in prison, and yet he was encouraging his friends to trust in God's powerful presence and peace to keep them through the difficult days they were going through, is astounding in itself. To the objective observer, peace is the last emotion in the world Paul *should* have been feeling, but the apostle knew from experience what he was talking about. He had suffered shipwreck and been stoned and lashed on several occasions—all because he was a follower of Jesus. And the one foundational truth he knew was that God's peace, though mysterious and impossible to comprehend rationally, is able to see anyone through the journey of life—on a routine day or in the midst of any trial.

There are many things that are like that in life. I'm grateful that I don't need to know all the intricate details of how my automobile works in order to be able to drive it to work. I'm grateful that I don't need to know all the processes involved in manufacturing in order to use various appliances. God's peace is functional in us—it is operative in us and available to us—far beyond our ability to understand it. God's promise of peace is a gift beyond compare.

3. God's Peace Is Extended to All His Followers

Is peace given to just a few? Is it a personality trait that only a select group of people have from birth? Or is peace available to all? The answer is clear. His plan includes everyone who chooses to trust and follow Him. But we also know that not everyone lives in a peaceful home environment, or in a neighborhood marked by peaceful coexistence among different races or cultures. Not every believer lives in a nation that is free of war, social struggles, or political conflict.

God's peace, however, is extended to *every* person who accepts Jesus as his or her Savior, turns from his or her sin, and pursues a life in obedience to the guidance of God's Word and the Holy Spirit.

Peace is a promise of God, and as mentioned before, the promises of God are for women and men of all ages, in all cultures, in all nations, throughout all generations. God does not give promises and then take them back. He does not offer a gift and then fail to deliver it. His promise of peace is for you!

The Bible has more than three hundred verses about peace. From cover to cover, God's Word presents the resounding truth: God wants you to be at peace with Him, and through your peace with Him, to have peace within your own heart, and as much as it depends upon your actions, to be at peace with your neighbors.

4. God's Peace Is Intended to Be an Abiding State of Being

Is peace elusive to you? Does it seem to come and go?

When was the last time you remember experiencing deep

26

peace in your heart? How long did that time of peace last? Why did you lose your peace?

Is your peace related only to an occasional spiritual high?

Have you concluded that, for you, peace in our perturbed world is a rare occurrence? Have you decided that you can't expect to be peaceful. You don't seek peace because you don't want to be disappointed when you fail to find it?

Can peace be an attitude, experience, and joy in your life that is there *most* of the time?

As I have asked these questions of various people throughout the last several years, I have discovered that most people think of peace as being very fleeting. It is not a "constant" in their lives.

The Greek word for peace means to "bind together" something that has been broken or disjointed. I think this is a superb illustration for how alienated men and women—so often feeling empty and disconnected from each other and God—can find a way to unity and wholeness. God's peace comes to them when they are united by faith with God.

This Greek word also refers to a prevailing sense of quietness and rest in a person's heart and emotions—of being unperturbed and unruffled. Peace is synonymous with being tranquil, serene, untroubled, and calm. It is a very real "state" of the soul.

You may be thinking, *Dr. Stanley, do you mean to tell me that I am never to be shocked or caught off guard by a sudden tragedy or time of trouble?* No, I'm not saying that. Trouble can come upon us so quickly that it catches us off guard. Our immediate response may be panic, anxiety, and fear. The person of peace, however, quickly feels a power rising up inside and regaining control at the helm of his life. That power is the Holy Spirit Himself, who speaks peace to the human heart, assuring the believer, "I'm here. I'm still in charge. Nothing is beyond My strength or My understanding. I'm with you. Don't be afraid."

The followers of Jesus are not immune from circumstances that are trying or disturbing. The promise to them is that the Holy Spirit is present to help, so a problem need not throw them off base or into a tailspin. A problem can be just a "blip" on the scope of your life. Peace—deep, genuine, God-given peace—can be the "norm" in which you live day to day.

If you feel peace only in spurts—for example, only on weekends, vacations, or on breaks—you are living your life different from the way God intended. God's desire is that you feel an abiding peace all the time, a peace that includes joy and a feeling of purpose in every area of your life—with times of anxiety or frustration being the "spurts" that occasionally hit us in crisis moments.

Plain and simple, a troubled soul is not God's desired norm for you, a heart anchored in peace is.

> **God's desire is that you feel an abiding peace all the time, a peace that includes joy and a feeling of purpose in every area of your life—with times of anxiety or frustration being the "spurts" that occasionally hit us in crisis moments.**

FOUR

WHY WE LOSE OUR PEACE

There is only one way to experience an abiding peace that transcends circumstances. The answer is "by faith." By faith we ask and then trust God to be present in our lives. It is as though we have put a sum of money in the bank, and by faith we write checks because we know that there are funds already deposited to cover our withdrawals. We have asked God to accept and forgive us and to be present in our lives with His abiding peace, and then we go out and live expecting Him to do the very thing we trust Him to do.

So the foundation for living in God's peace is faith—an active, confident trust in His presence and power to sustain and comfort you no matter what the circumstance you face. There are, however, certain issues that can rob us of our peace. Let me mention a few of them:

1. SUDDEN FEAR

Here's a sweet story told to me by a woman who learned this truth the hard way:

When she was a child, her mother had prepared her for the

first day of kindergarten. Her mother had taken her to the school and shown her the classroom. She had introduced her to her teacher. She had walked her to the bus stop where the bus would pick her up and drop her off in the afternoon.

My friend said, "On the first day of school, my mother said to me before she walked me to the bus stop, 'Remember, Jesus is right there with you all day. He knows right where you are.' And then she added, almost as an afterthought, 'He knows where you need to be, and He will help you get there.'

"Well," my friend said, "when the school bus pulled up to the school, it drove right past the kindergarten rooms. I could see my classroom, and as soon as I got off the bus, I headed toward it. I didn't get more than a few steps before a teacher stopped me. She said, 'You can't go that way.'

"I said, 'But I can see my room.' The teacher said, 'No, you have to go this way to get there.' She pointed in the opposite direction from the classroom to a fairly large group of students who were walking together. She nudged me toward them.

"I had no idea where I was. Mom hadn't shown me that part of the school. I was just a little girl in a very big group of children walking down one hallway and then the next. I was scared. I kept saying to myself, 'Jesus is right here with me. Jesus knows where I am. He knows where I need to be, and He's going to help me get there.' I kept saying those sentences over and over as I kept walking.

"Along the way groups of students left the main hallway and went to various classrooms. I was more and more confused, but I kept walking with the main group of students. Finally there were only a few of us still walking together. The others were third graders, and when they turned away from the main hallway to go to their rooms, I found myself walking alone, still saying to myself, 'Jesus is right here with me. Jesus knows where I am. He knows where I need to be, and He's going to help me get there.'

"I looked up . . . and there was my room and my teacher! I was never so relieved in all my life!

"The next day, I had a little more confidence. I *knew* Jesus was with me and He knew where I was, and He would help me get to my room. I had peace. By the end of the first week, I had the routine learned!"

And then my friend said these words I'll never forget: "People all my life have asked me why I seem to be so confident, even in situations I've never experienced before, including some scary and troubling times. I think it goes back to that first day of school. Mom told me that Jesus was right there with me. She told me Jesus knew where I was, knew where I was supposed to be, and that Jesus would help me. I didn't doubt her. I believed in the truth of God's presence with me, and I never stopped believing.

"I've walked down the hallways of life with peace and confidence ever since. I may feel a little lost at times. I may not know all I should know. But I know that I'm connected to the Way and the Truth, and He'll get me to where He knows I'm supposed to be."

There's the truth in a nutshell. She kept remembering her mother's words and trusted that Jesus was there to help her and give her peace—in spite of the fear she felt so strongly as she sought to navigate in a big, strange place.

Some people are so accustomed to responding to every little dip and rise of life with fear and small doses of panic that they can't even imagine there's another way to respond. They are so upset by change of all types that it never even dawns on them that they can live with greater emotional stability.

Say no to fear. Instead, practice a life of trust. Every day begin with the affirmation, "I trust You, Jesus. I count on Your peace and presence today."

2. THE ENEMY

We can be attacked by our enemy, the devil, who may use various means to cause us to doubt and lose faith in our God. He often does this by priming the pump of doubt with questions— for example, "If God is with you, then why has this happened?" On occasions like this, you have to stand up to the devil, the one who is the ultimate source of any fear that paralyzes you or any anxiety that lingers and hinders you.

I sometimes speak out loud to the devil, the evil power that seeks to thwart the plan of God in our lives. I tell him forthrightly, "Devil, you will *not* have my peace. I refuse to live in fear and worry. I *will* trust God." In the Scriptures, we are urged to resist the devil, and when we do, he *must* flee from us (see James 4:7). So, at moments of fear and anxiousness, resist him in the name of Jesus!

3. SIN

It is very important for us to repent of any sin that may become an obstacle to our receiving and enjoying the peace of God. Check your own heart for any sin that may be resident— anything that counteracts God's peace. Sin always creates such an obstacle.

A person can pray repeatedly for God's peace and believe in his heart for God's peace. He can remind himself of the promises of God and quote them too. But if that person continues to harbor sin in his life and willfully chooses to continue to rebel against God, he will not experience true peace. Even what seems to be a simple matter, like not forgiving someone who offended you, can create havoc in your spirit. The convicting power of the Holy Spirit will continue to *compel* you to face up to what you know is a sin before God. And until you do so, you will have a restlessness and anxiety deep within. The more a person asks God for peace, the more that inner turmoil is likely to increase.

Peace and rebellion cannot coexist!

The only recourse is to confess the rebellion to God, surrender that area of life to Him, and ask Him for help in turning away from that sin and resisting all temptation to return to it. Then God's peace can flow in your life again.

4. Giving Up Peace

So often in times of crisis we lay down our peace. Yes, we actually give it over to someone else. I had what for me was a very traumatic incident some time ago. I remember the incident well. As I came to my car, it was evident that someone had broken into it, and my briefcase was missing. "No! No! No!" The words came out of my mouth almost involuntarily. I could hardly believe what I was seeing—the front seat was empty and one of my most precious possessions was gone.

My briefcase contained my Greek New Testament, which I felt fairly certain the robber could not read, and a couple of other books and papers that were probably insignificant to the thief. All those items were fairly easy to replace, and I felt very little pain over the loss. The briefcase itself was fairly old, so I didn't feel much pain over its loss either, but what pained me was this: In my briefcase was my favorite Bible. It was the one I had preached from for years. I had marked various notes and dates throughout the Bible. It was something of a biographical sketch of the way the Lord had spoken to me through the years. I felt as if a major "record" of my life had been taken.

And that wasn't all. The Bible had been a gift from my mother.

For about three months, I felt as if I had lost my best friend. I wasn't angry as much as I felt grieved. Someone had intruded into my life—including my spiritual life—and had taken something very valuable to me. In moments like this—moments of loss, of unwarranted accusation against your character, or of personal rejection—it is so easy to fall into the trap of losing your peace.

On a number of occasions through the years when I have felt troubled, anxious, or frustrated, I blamed other people for "stealing" my peace. I was wrong. The truth is, nobody else should ever have been blamed for my loss of peace. In each and every case, I was the one who laid it down.

Hear me very carefully on this point. Nobody can take your peace from you. If you have lost your peace, you have lost it for one main reason—you have surrendered it.

Nobody can take your peace from you. If you have lost your peace, you have lost it for one main reason—you have surrendered it.

Time and again I hear people say that they are distressed or troubled in spirit by something that happened or something that was said or done against them. I hear variations of "if only she," "if only he," and "if only circumstances had been different" statements. Again, the truth is that no circumstance, situation, person, or organization can steal your inner peace.

We lose our peace because we lay it down. We give it up. We concede it. We abandon it.

5. LOSING FOCUS

We can allow the myriad of bad-news situations we hear and read about every day to cause us to lose our correct focus. Instead of having our minds set on God and trusting Him for His peace and presence, we allow our thoughts to get sidetracked and galvanized by the negative news and circumstances we see and hear.

Just think about the last twelve months. Do you recall the story of thirteen miners who died at a mine in Brookwood, Alabama? After an initial explosion in the mine, three miners were trapped. Ten other miners immediately went into the mine to attempt a rescue. While seeking to give aid to their friends, another explosion claimed their lives. Wives had sent their husbands to work that morning and had never seen them again.

Do you remember the massive earthquakes that struck both Turkey and Italy? Thousands went to bed one evening and never saw the dawn of the next day. What about the shootings in our schools and the recent sniper attacks across the United States?

I recall hearing from a friend about a man and his wife who had gone on a long-awaited vacation together. While they were fly-fishing, a storm arose. The husband went to the car in the driving rain, but the wife decided to stay under the shelter of a large tree where it was drier. Lightning struck the tree and killed her instantly. What began as a fun outing together ended tragically.

And of course, we all remember the first images we saw of the collapsing World Trade Center towers in New York City, the gaping hole ablaze at the Pentagon in Washington, D.C., and the debris scattered in a field in Pennsylvania. Hundreds of men, women, and children boarded planes that morning and never arrived at their intended destinations. Thousands of families waited for horror-stricken hours, days, weeks, and some even until now for any physical remains of their relatives to come home for burial.

Coping with the news of some kind of tragedy seems to have become part of our daily agenda. A deep sense of foreboding and fearful anticipation seems to hang over our nation. It isn't always major events, however; bad news may be far less dramatic than the instances I've noted above, but the events can still be just as threatening to us.

We may hear bad news from a physician about our health or the health of a loved one. We may hear bad news about a couple that has separated or divorced, about a child who has run away, about a job that has been lost, or a financial enterprise that has filed for bankruptcy. When we see and hear of such terrible news, it is so easy for us to become focused on the negative, to become paralyzed by fear, and sometimes to project that some of these negative possibilities could happen to us so we, too, may become victims. Let me suggest some things for you to consider if you feel your peace is slipping away or you have become focused on the negative aspects of life:

Question #1: Have you stopped thanking and praising God? People who lay down their peace often have stopped praying with thanksgiving and praise. Followers of Jesus need a vibrant prayer life. As the gospel song says, they need to "stay in touch with God." They must avoid talking with God only about what they think they need, and regularly live with a thankful heart—giving thanks always in all circumstances for all things. There is a direct correlation between the degree people pray with faith, praise, and thanksgiving, and their confidence in prayer, their assurance that God hears and answers their cries to Him.

Question #2: Are you limiting God by the way you think? Imagine a circumstance that you consider to be bad. Use whatever descriptive words you want to use—hard, difficult, agonizing, strenuous, debilitating, horrific, sorrowful, perturbing, penetrating, or painful. Is there a problem too awful or too hard for God to handle?

If your answer to this question is anything other than "no," your understanding of God is too limited or small. The well-known devotional writer Oswald Chambers wrote, "When it begins to dawn on my conscious life what God's purpose is, there is the laughter of the possibility of the impossible. The impossible is exactly what God does." He had it right. With God the impossible is possible, so there is nothing too big for our God. We do not want to be charged with having a God that's too small, do we?

Our God is a *great* and *limitless* God. He dwells in eternity and operates in infinity. He has *all* things within His understanding and *all* things under His control.

Question #3: Are you dwelling on negatives? Most people who lay down their peace later admit they had begun dwelling on the negative aspects of life. Rather they should have harnessed their minds to dwell on and appreciate the positive, good things of life.

The temptation to dwell on the negative aspects of life is profound. I mentioned earlier how debilitating this can be to the life of our souls. Interestingly, this tendency to negatively focus is often begun in our homes and institutions—fathers criticizing their children with little or no praise to balance their assessment, supervisors telling their employees what they are doing wrong far more than telling them what they are doing right— the same is true for teachers, doctors, lawyers, and accountants. Much of the information these professionals give us tends to deal with errors, negative situations, breaches of law, and numbers that cannot be reconciled.

It is not uncommon for a person to go through an entire day and not hear one encouraging statement from another human being.

If you feed your heart and mind a continual diet of negativity, your faith will begin to erode. If you do the same with those with whom you live and work, they, too, will become negative, self-deprecating, and critical of themselves and others. This is what you and they will be thinking and saying:

"What's the use?"

"Why try?"

"Nothing goes my way."

"The world is going to pieces."

"Nothing is secure or safe anymore."

"People are just out to get me."

The more a person thinks along any of these lines, the more depressed, distressed, and oppressed that person is likely to feel!

Question #4: Are you allowing negative emotions to linger in your heart? There are times when we are hit from the blind side by an accident, tragedy, sickness, or undesirable situation. There are also the internal impulses and desires that can cause us twinges of inner anguish or need. There are times when we suddenly find ourselves in a difficult situation that we had not anticipated. There are moments when we hear or see devastating news that causes us momentarily to feel as if the rug has been pulled out from under our feet.

Anxiety occurs. Panic erupts. Fear strikes.

When those moments occur, we can do one of two things. We can either open the door and invite those negative, unproductive emotions to settle into our hearts, or we can take action immediately to regain our peace and confidence!

Now, anxiety, panic, and fear are *normal* human responses to a sudden accident, tragedy, crisis, a deeply unsettling situation, or bad news. These responses are nearly instinctual. They are "automatic." There is no fault in *feeling* these emotions. They are part of God's built-in warning system to us so we might take action to seek protection or preservation of life. They are something of a fight-or-flee reaction to what we perceive to be threatening. Every person feels moments of anxiety, panic, or fear at times.

The error comes when we *accept* these emotions, whether with open arms or begrudgingly, and allow them to linger and gradually find a resting place in our hearts. If we do that, these emotions become chronic or long lasting. They become our "state of being," not just a temporary response. They become our prevailing attitude and mind-set. Rather than allowing negative "stuff" to capture our hearts, we need to do what Jesus did and taught.

Question #5: Are you forgetting Jesus' example? I find it fascinating that Jesus, our Master, was a realist. Jesus never called those who followed Him to live in denial or to live with their heads in the sand. To the contrary, throughout the Gospels Jesus confronted problems. He acknowledged the fierce temptations of the devil and the controlling power of sin at work in the world. He didn't take His disciples off to a monastery in a remote place to escape the world. No! He called His disciples to be "in the world" and yet not "of the world"—in other words, not to be ruled by the world's evil systems or governed by human tendencies.

> Jesus, our Master, was a realist. Jesus never called those who followed Him to live in denial or to live with their heads in the sand.

Jesus knew He and His disciples were living in a troublesome time. He called them to face trouble head-on, but He called them to do it by following His example. So He told them not to keep worrying about tomorrow—whether they would have clothes to wear or sufficient food to eat. He reminded His followers that their heavenly Father looked after the sparrows and clothed the "lilies of the field" and He would, no doubt, do the same for them!

The assurance of Jesus is that because God is with us, we do not have to give in to, sink beneath, or become defeated by troubles. We can face them, confront them, challenge them, deal with them, and in the end overcome them! What consolation this should bring to our hearts.

Jesus taught His followers that all troubles are passing in nature. Sickness and trouble are for a season and for a reason. Storms arose and prevailed—both in the natural on the Sea of Galilee and in the supernatural lives of those possessed and oppressed by the devil—for a season and a reason. Jesus' very life was for a season and a reason. Even His death and burial in a tomb were only for a season and a reason!

The passing nature of troubles is something Jesus calls us to recognize. His challenge is to endure, to persevere, to learn, to grow, and to overcome. I use the little phrase "for a season and a reason" because I think it explains accurately the issue. Jesus knew that God permits things to happen in our lives only for a certain period of time and for a particular reason.

I believe an even more accurate way of translating His "Let not your heart be troubled" would be "Don't let your heart be troubled any longer." And why should we be troubled and lose our peace if we remember our Lord's example of living confidently knowing that His Father was watching, directing, caring for, and loving Him and His followers on a daily basis? God will do the same for us.

FIVE ESSENTIAL BELIEFS FOR A PEACEFUL HEART

D o you think Saddam Hussein or Osama bin Laden or any other person on this earth is in control of your safety and well-being? If so, you are sorely mistaken. If you are a Christian, then God alone is in charge of your life. He is your security.

"But what about the events of September 11, 2001?" you may ask. "Was God in control?"

My answer is, "Absolutely!" God has never been out of control over His creation for one fraction of a second since the beginning of time. Could God have prevented what happened? Certainly. Did God *allow* what happened? Yes. Did He have a purpose for allowing this to happen to our nation? Without a doubt.

> **God has never been out of control over His creation for one fraction of a second since the beginning of time.**

We may not completely understand God's purposes, but we can be assured of this—God is *still* in control. He hasn't lost one measure of His power or might. He is just as omnipotent, omniscient, omnipresent, and all loving today as He was the day before September 11, 2001.

The godly response to tragedies such as those that occurred 9/11 are not the questions "Why did this happen?" or "Why did God allow this?" The godly response is to ask, "God, what do You want me to learn in response to this?"

If you continue to ask why, you will get bogged down, because why questions can never be answered fully. If you begin to ask, "What now?" or "How shall I respond?" you will find yourself moving forward with direction, purpose, and new energy. You will also have much greater peace.

Understanding the ways of God always leads to an understanding that God will act in a way that brings about eternal blessings for His children. It is what we *believe* that makes it possible to ask the right questions in the face of a tragedy.

Through the years I have discovered five essential beliefs for a peaceful heart. I challenge you to take a long, hard look at what *you* believe about God. Your peace is determined by the degree to which these truths are embedded in your soul.

ESSENTIAL BELIEF #1:
GOD IS ABSOLUTELY SOVEREIGN

Recognizing and accepting the truth that God is sovereign over absolutely everything is vital for your inner peace. God is absolutely sovereign—which means that nothing related to you is beyond His watchful eye and loving care.

So many people live with a nagging concern: "What will happen? Suppose this happens? Suppose that happens?" I've met a large number of people in just the last two years who tell me that they have a gnawing fear deep within—they wonder what will happen if they get on an airplane, open their mail, go into a high-rise building, or are bitten by a disease-carrying mosquito or tick. Others have confessed to me that they have a daily fear of sending their children to school. Still others have admitted they have a fearful dread of opening the business section of their newspaper—they feel an ongoing pressure inside them about the stock market and the current business climate.

If you have any of these concerns, I encourage you to carefully read Psalm 91—one of the outstanding passages in the Bible—as it speaks about God's control over all the affairs of life. It reads:

He who dwells in the secret place of the Most High
Shall abide under the shadow of the Almighty.
I will say of the LORD, "He is my refuge and my fortress;
My God, in Him I will trust."
Surely He shall deliver you from the snare of the fowler
And from the perilous pestilence.
He shall cover you with His feathers,
And under His wings you shall take refuge;
His truth shall be your shield and buckler.
You shall not be afraid of the terror by night,
Nor of the arrow that flies by day,
Nor of the pestilence that walks in darkness,
Nor of the destruction that lays waste at noonday.
A thousand may fall at your side,
And ten thousand at your right hand;

But it shall not come near you.

Only with your eyes shall you look,

And see the reward of the wicked.

Because you have made the LORD, who is my refuge,

Even the Most High, your dwelling place,

No evil shall befall you,

Nor shall any plague come near your dwelling;

For He shall give His angels charge over you,

To keep you in all your ways.

In their hands they shall bear you up,

Lest you dash your foot against a stone.

You shall tread upon the lion and the cobra,

The young lion and the serpent you shall trample underfoot.

"Because he has set his love upon Me, therefore I will deliver him;

I will set him on high, because he has known My name.

He shall call upon Me, and I will answer him;

I will be with him in trouble;

I will deliver him and honor him.

With long life I will satisfy him,

And show him My salvation."

God is your protector. He is the One who preserves your life from hour to hour, day to day, year to year. He is in charge of keeping you alive on this earth until the split second that He desires for you to be in eternity with Him. No matter what happens to you, God has a plan to bless you on this earth and reward you in eternity. Everything you experience, even those things that you might label "bad," God can and will turn to eternal good if you will only trust Him to be your sovereign Lord.

A friend recently received very upsetting news in the mail. The realty company that had handled the sale of a house he owned was being sued by the couple who had purchased the house. The buyers were claiming fraud, and the implication was that my friend had been deceitful in what he had failed to disclose about the condition of the home at the time of the sale, as well as negligent in making repairs. While my friend was not named in the lawsuit against the realty company, he nonetheless was shocked at the allegations made against the real-estate agent and, indirectly, against him. For a few moments, he felt uneasy, sick at heart, and confused as to what course of action to take. His peace was momentarily shattered.

He told me, "Then as I finished reading the text of this legal document for the second time, I remembered you saying in a sermon, 'God is in control. He's always in control.' So I prayed, 'Lord, You are in control. This letter isn't any surprise to You. You know my heart. You know that I dealt honestly and in a straightforward way with this couple. You know that I disclosed everything that I knew to be a problem with the property I sold. You know that I did my best to comply with all the rules and regulations stipulated by both the realty company and the property inspectors. You know how much money I spent on the required repairs, and that I went above and beyond what was required legally, both in disclosure and in fixing up the property for this family. I ask You right now to help me know what to do and how to respond, including whether I should do anything at all. Show me how to pray for this couple. Show me how to pray for the real-estate agent.'"

"What happened?" I asked.

He said, "I immediately had peace fill my heart. I knew without any doubt that I wasn't to do anything but pray for the couple that had purchased the house. I had a deep knowing that this couple had needs that were far deeper and more eternal in importance than the superficial property-upkeep needs that were outlined in the long letter they had written to the realty company. They were troubled, overwhelmed, in a panic, seeking to blame others, and were perhaps undercapitalized for the purchase they had made. So I set myself to praying that God would meet their needs and turn their hearts. I knew that if they continued to pursue this lawsuit, they were going to find themselves even more frustrated, more hurt, and that they very likely would not receive more than a small portion of the compensation they were seeking. As best I could tell from other property transactions I've been through, this sale had been handled in a quality manner.

"I don't know what will ultimately happen in this case," this friend concluded, "but I do know this. God is in control. He knows my heart, my motives, and all that has happened. He will protect me. And I also believe He will fulfill His purposes in the lives of this couple and the lives of all who are involved with this case at the realty company."

"Do you know why you have this confidence and peace?" I asked.

"Sure," he said with a smile. "You're just testing me, aren't you? I have peace because God said He would work all things together for good to those who are the called according to His purpose. I was led by God to sell this property. I sold it in a godly manner and with a clear conscience in all aspects of the sale. God will be true to His Word. All things will work together for good."

He was absolutely right.

Essential Belief #2:
God Is Your Provider

From cover to cover, the Bible has a clear message that God is the One who provides for all your needs. No need is too massive, too problematic, or too severe for Jesus to meet it! The Bible tells us: "Those who seek the LORD shall not lack any good thing" (Ps. 34:10).

It is not part of God's plan for you to lie awake at night, tossing and turning and wondering, *How am I going to pay my bills if I lose my job? What am I going to do when I retire if the stock market continues to decline? How am I going to provide for my family if my company goes through bankruptcy?* or any other concern that you may have.

The need you have may not be a need for food, water, or clothing. It may be a need for emotional healing, spiritual deliverance, a new opportunity for employment, reconciliation of a broken relationship, or any one of a host of other internal or relational needs. Friend, God is able to meet that need! He is the God who provides for His people all things that are required for a full, satisfying, and purposeful life.

Jesus said,

I am the door of the sheep. All who ever came before Me are thieves and robbers, but the sheep did not hear them. I am the door. If anyone enters by Me, he will be saved, and will go in and out and find pasture. The thief does not come except to steal, and to kill, and to destroy. I have come that they may have life, and that they may have it more abundantly. (John 10:7–10)

Jesus was referring to the fact that in Bible times, shepherds slept with their sheep when the sheep spent the night in outdoor pens that were made of rocks. The shepherd would lie in the open doorway that allowed the sheep to enter the pen. With his very life, the shepherd would protect the sheep from any predators or thieves. Note that Jesus said that we are not only saved because Jesus stands between us and the enemy who seeks to steal, kill, and destroy us, but that Jesus, as our Shepherd, allows us to "find pasture." That little two-word phrase means that a sheep has all of its needs for survival met fully.

Not only does Jesus provide eternal life when we accept Him as our Savior, but He also came to provide us an abundant life. An abundant life is a life filled to overflowing with every good blessing so we can accomplish all the Lord has called us to do and to be in our lives.

If you lose your job, God has another job for you. As you trust Him to lead you and to open the doors for you, that new job will be a better opportunity.

If you have been relying on one source of income to provide the money you need to pay your bills and that source of income changes, God has countless other means of providing for you.

Never forget that God

- sent manna to feed more than two million Israelites who were wandering in a wilderness—in fact, He sent manna for decades to meet their need for food (Ex. 16:35).

- brought forth water out of solid rock to give life-giving refreshment to His people (Ex. 17:6).

- sent ravens with food to feed His prophet Elijah even in a time of terrible drought and famine (1 Kings 17:4–6).

- multiplied a boy's sack lunch of bread and fish to feed thousands of people (Matt. 14:14–21).

- provided a daily supply of oil and flour for the prophet Elijah and a single mother—in fact, this supply lasted for years until a time of famine came to an end (1 Kings 17:10–16).

- multiplied a supply of oil for a widow after the death of her husband so she could support herself and her sons (2 Kings 4:1–7).

The examples of provision in the Bible are too numerous to recount fully. If you doubt God's ability to provide for you, remind yourself of the many methods He has used to provide for His people. Remember as you read about His provision that God is the same today as He was in Bible times. His nature as your Provider is unwavering. His resources are unlimited. His love for you is infinite. And His power to provide is absolute.

You cannot have peace and at the same time doubt that God will provide for you. Settle the issue once and for all in your heart and mind. God is your Provider. He will meet your needs as you learn to trust and obey Him.

Trust God in all financial matters! Do you believe God is in control of your finances? Are you certain that you are handling your finances the way God wants you to handle them?

If you can answer yes to those questions, then you need to put down your worries and get on with the business at hand—continue to use your money and manage your finances in a godly way. Focus your work at those things that God has put in your path to do, and help others to the best of your ability. God has ways and means of providing for you that you haven't even dreamed about.

> **You cannot have peace and at the same time doubt that God will provide for you. Settle the issue once and for all in your heart and mind. God is your Provider.**

Ask yourself "Who is in control of my material resources?" If you think you are in control, you're wrong. You certainly have a responsibility to be a good steward, or manager, of the resources God has given to you . . . but you aren't in control of your income or the material substance that comes your way. Everything you have today is a gift from God to you. He is the One who has given you the energy, vitality, health, ideas, and opportunities that have led to your "possessing" all that you have. Surely as He has provided for you all your life, He will continue to provide for you as you trust Him, obey Him, and seek to do His will.

If the stock market is the governing force for your material resources, you are in trouble. If your financial future is based upon your own human ability to "figure out" the wisest investments, you are in trouble. It is only as God gives you wisdom that you can make sound financial choices in today's marketplace. Ask God to guide you. Ask Him to reveal to you if there is anything about the way you are presently handling your material resources that should be changed.

If you don't have peace in a particular area of your finances or possessions, ask God to reveal to you where you should be investing your finances. He will reveal ways in which you should be handling your resources so you can experience His peace.

I recently heard about a woman who suddenly had no peace about living in the home she had occupied for more than fifty years. She had a great urgency to be out of her house, not just for an afternoon, but to sell it and move. She put her house on the market, and to her amazement, the real-estate agent she contacted told her that her house was worth far more than she thought. Furthermore, she learned that a temple was going to be built only about a half mile from her home. Apparently, members of this religion wanted to live close to this temple and they were the ones who were driving the prices so high. She realized even as the real-estate agent gave her this information that most of her neighborhood would likely be filled with families who had a membership in that temple in a relatively short time. This loomed as a problem for this dear woman. She was single, mature in age, and felt concern about being alienated from her longtime neighbors and friends.

Now, as soon as her daughter and son-in-law heard that she was willing to move, they invited her to come live with them. They had wanted this for years, but hadn't pushed the issue since she had been so adamant about keeping her house and living in it until the day she died. She accepted their invitation, and within two months, she had sold her home and moved. For the next ten years of her life, she lived in great comfort and peace, receiving the love and tender attention of her daughter, son-in-law, and four grandchildren.

Was God in charge of this woman's financial matters? Did He

provide for her? Exceedingly and abundantly more than she could ever have asked or imagined (Eph. 3:20)!

ESSENTIAL BELIEF #3:
GOD MADE YOU THE WAY YOU ARE
FOR A PURPOSE

There are many things about your life in which you have no control. Accept those things as part of the way God made you. A friend of mine recently said, "God gave me fair skin. My skin seems to turn red even when I think about being out in the sun. I'd love to have a nice dark tan, but it's just not the way God made me. So . . . I put on sunscreen, wear my straw hat, wear loose, long-sleeved clothing, and go to sunny places anyway. Just because God didn't create me with the ability to tan doesn't mean He does not want me to enjoy a tropical island!" This woman has accepted the way God made her.

Another friend said to me years ago, "I don't know why God made me so short and gave me such dark hair and dark skin. I'm by far the shortest person in my family, and my skin and hair are darker than the skin and hair of any of my brothers and sisters. But the way God designed me sure makes my work as a missionary in Mexico easier." I laughed and said, "God saw you working as a missionary in Mexico long before your birth. Don't you realize that's why He made you the way He did?"

Your race, culture, language, nationality, sex, and many attributes of your physical being are God's "choices." God also gave you certain talents and aptitudes that make it easier for you to acquire and perfect certain skills. He gave you a degree of intelligence to develop through study and to apply to practical matters. He gave you a basic personality—even from birth some babies seem more outgoing and others seem more passive. At the time you accepted Jesus Christ as your Savior, God gave you certain spiritual gifts to use in ministry to others. The way in which you express those gifts is uniquely linked to the talents He has given you and the skills He has helped you develop.

You are a unique and very special creation of God, designed for a particular purpose on this earth that God has had in mind from eternity past. Accept who God made you to be!

All these traits and factors taken as a whole make you a unique person on this earth. Nobody who has ever lived before you has been just like you. Nobody alive on the earth today is just like you, not even a sibling who is your twin. Nobody who will ever live will be just like you, including your children. You are a unique and very special creation of God, designed for a particular purpose on this earth that God has had in mind from eternity past. Accept who God made you to be!

I've met people who are very upset with the ministry gifts God has given to them. A man once said to me, "God gave me a gift of mercy. Some people think I'm a wimp. I wish He had given me a gift of exhortation." To want a ministry gift other than the one God has given you is to say three things: "God, You made a mistake," "God, I don't like who You have called me to be," and "God, I'm not going to use this gift You've given me to the maximum of my ability." A person who doesn't value and appreciate his or her own ministry gift is a person who isn't eager to volunteer that gift or be willing to use the talent even when asked.

I've also met people who are very upset with the physical features God has given to them. Some people hate one aspect of their appearance to the point that they despise their whole being. Others don't like their appearance so much that they withdraw, isolating themselves from other people. Still others hate one aspect of their appearances so much that they seem bent on destroying all aspects of their appearances—they let themselves go completely.

I'm not opposed to the use of makeup, hair stylists, or even plastic surgery. But I am deeply concerned about people who dislike their appearance so much that they turn away from God because they blame Him for the way He made them. Some go to extreme measures in improving their appearance to the point where they spend virtually all their money and much of their time on improving their image. Some withdraw from serving God openly and willingly because they are too preoccupied with what they perceive to be their less-than-attractive appearance, physical handicap or limitation, or physical weakness. They are missing out on much of the joy God desires for them to experience in life. They certainly don't have peace deep within their hearts.

CHANGE WHAT YOU CAN CHANGE

If you look at yourself in the mirror and conclude, "I'd like my appearance better if I lost twenty pounds," then lose those pounds. Don't moan and groan about how many fat cells God gave you. Make some decisions about how to drain those cells of their fat. On the other hand, don't look at yourself in the mirror and conclude, "I'd sure like to be six inches taller." That wish isn't going to come true no matter what you do!

What do you say when you look at yourself in the morning? Is it, "Yech!" or do you laugh and say, "Well, there are some improvements I could make here," or do you say, "Hmmm. Not bad!" Each of us should get to the point at which we say, "I'm getting better every day!"

God expects us to change whatever it takes to be our best at whatever we do. He wants us to look our best, dress our best, speak our best, act our best, try our best, give our best, and work to the best of our ability and energy. It is important to understand that the term *best* is related to your own potential, not a term of comparison with others. Your best has nothing to do with another person's best. Furthermore, your best today is not likely to be your best tomorrow. We all can improve certain aspects of our lives, and continue to improve them every day for the rest of our lives.

You will live up to the image that you have of yourself. Your actions will follow your imagination every time. If you see yourself as a failure, you will act like a failure, and in the end, you will fail.

If you see yourself as ugly, you will do very little to improve your appearance, and in the end, you will sink to the worst image you have of yourself.

If you see yourself as stupid, you won't study or learn to develop skills, you won't seek opportunities in which to apply what you do know, and you will remain as uneducated, inept, or undeveloped tomorrow as you are today.

The person you see yourself to be will in the end be the person you become.

NEVER STOP GROWING IN CHARACTER

One area in which God always challenges us to grow and change is in our character. The Bible tells us that God is at work in every believer's life to conform that person into the character likeness of Christ Jesus. The character that God desires for us to manifest bears the hallmark qualities of love, joy, peace, longsuffering, kindness, goodness, faithfulness, gentleness, and self-control (Gal. 5:22–23).

Everyone can always be more loving. Everyone can always have still greater joy, be more at peace, have greater patience, show more kindness, reflect more goodness, walk in greater faithfulness. They can express themselves with greater gentleness, and manifest more self-control. No matter how mature the believer, there's always room for growth in these areas. And there are always opportunities to display these traits in new situations, environments, and relationships.

Your flesh, your mind, your outer material possessions are not the most important aspects of the real you. True importance of you is bound up in your character.

You can't have enough money, you can't have enough friends, you can't take enough drugs or enough alcohol, you can't go enough places or have enough experiences, you can't lose enough weight or gain enough muscle, you can't wear expensive enough clothing and jewelry or drive a fancy enough car to ever compensate for a poor character.

REJECT LIES YOU MAY HAVE BEEN TOLD

I've discovered through the years that a very high percentage of people with a poor self-image acquired that self-image because of what someone said or did to them in their childhoods. In nearly all cases, somebody lied to them and they bought into the lie. Somebody told them, "You can't do that," "You'll never amount to anything," "You're not wanted," "You're not worthy," "You can't be successful," "You can't learn that," or "You can't become that." The truth is, somebody fed them an opinion that was not rooted in what God has said . . . and they believed the lie. They acted according to the lie. They "lived out" the failure that somebody predicted for their life.

Sometimes people who don't like themselves voice deep criticism of self, and at other times they try to gloss over what they don't like with little jokes. I've heard people of all ages say such things as, "There's nobody who cares anyway" or "I'm just stupid" or "Mama always said I'd fail at this" or "Dad was never there for me."

Those statements, while they may be rooted in fact, also are clues to a person's emotional well-being and self-image. Anyone who says, "Nobody cares," very likely believes the reason is: "There's no value in loving me." The person who says, "I'm just stupid," is voicing a belief that he is incapable of learning or is inadequate intellectually. The person who says, "Mama always said . . . ," is a person who has believed that he is unqualified for success. The person who says, "Dad was never there for me" is a person who internalized the belief that he was unworthy of Dad's love and attention. These are all signs that point to the conclusion: "I'm not lovable." That's a lie! God says you are lovable!

Take stock of what you have been told about yourself. Were you told the truth? If you have in any way been taught a lie about yourself—which is something contrary to what God says about you—

then it is up to you to reject what you have been told and believe what God's Word says about you. You are lovable. You are worthy. You are intelligent and talented. God has created you to succeed.

ACCEPT THE TRUTH OTHERS SPEAK TO YOU

Other people have been told a truth about themselves that they have refused to believe. Thousands of young women across our nation believe they are overweight and are struggling with anorexia nervosa, bulimia, and other eating disorders—many have refused to believe parents, teachers, doctors, and close friends who have told them repeatedly that they are not overweight. They have refused to accept the truth about themselves.

If someone says to you, "You look fantastic today," don't dismiss his or her comment. Accept in that person's eyes that you do look fantastic!

If someone says to you, "You're really smart" or "You're really creative," don't dismiss their compliment with self-deprecating remarks or a comment that sweeps aside their assessment of you. Agree with the person! You are smart to some degree, in some ways. You are creative to some degree, in some ways. And the person who gives you that compliment is trying to express appreciation for who you are. Accept the compliment and that you are being appreciated!

At times a person will respond to a compliment with a "thank you," but the minute he walks away, he says to himself, "He doesn't really mean that. He's just saying that. I wish he wouldn't say things like that." If you find yourself thinking such thoughts after you receive a compliment, take note. There's something about yourself that you aren't valuing or appreciating.

A surgeon once told me about a patient of his who was in a terrible automobile accident. The victim was a beautiful teenage girl. The accident horribly mangled her face. After several years and several surgeries, everybody who saw that young woman thought she was even more beautiful than she had been before the accident. But the girl herself still saw a mangled, disfigured face when she looked in the mirror. She refused to believe the truth that others frequently spoke to her. She discounted every compliment and actually became angry when a person said, "You're very beautiful."

This surgeon said, "It wasn't until a total stranger at church spoke to her one day that she began to change her self-image. This person was praying with her and she said, 'The Lord has just spoken to my heart that I'm to tell you something.' The young woman said, 'What is it?' The woman praying with her said, 'The Lord wants you to know that He thinks you are beautiful and He wants you to start thinking about yourself the way He thinks about you.' That young woman began to weep. She didn't stop crying for hours. Believing the truth about herself was a hard thing for her to accept, but once she did, she was able to let go of the bitterness and anger she had held on to in the aftermath of her accident. Believing the truth brought about a healing deep inside her, even though the injuries to her face had healed long before."

Do you have the courage to lay down the lies you have been told and to receive God's truth about your life? Do you have the courage to walk in that truth?

Accept who God created you to be. Change what you know you can change, need to change, or God is asking you to change.

Trade in the lies of others for God's truth about you. Be willing to continue to yield to the conforming work of the Holy Spirit and to develop the character He desires for you to develop.

And friend, you will have greater peace deep within.

ESSENTIAL BELIEF #4:
GOD HAS A PLACE WHERE
YOU TRULY BELONG

A person who feels unwanted, rejected, or continually lonely is not a person who has peace deep within. Feeling that we belong to someone or to a group of people who love us is vital for our inner peace.

Everybody on earth wants to be loved and to love someone. When you feel as if you are connected to someone who appreciates you, values you, and loves you, you have feelings of deep tranquillity and calm.

God tells us plainly that we are to have fellowship with other believers in the church. The Bible clearly tells us that we are not to forsake the assembling of ourselves together (Heb. 10:25). Why? Because every person in the body of Christ has been given a unique personality, set of abilities and skills, at least one ministry gift, and natural talents. God expects each of us to share these unique attributes with other believers in a loving, generous way so needs within any particular body of believers will be met and the gospel will be extended to those outside the church. We need one another in the church. We are part of one another.

At the church I pastor, we have members who represent more than fifty nations. What a warm fellowship we have!

You may not go to a church as large or diverse, but in a sense, you do belong to such a church—as believers in Christ, we are all part of the same body of Christ that encompasses the entire world. The Holy Spirit connects you to believers everywhere. The apostle Paul wrote, "There is neither Jew nor Greek, there is neither slave nor free, there is neither male nor female; for you are all one in Christ Jesus. And if you are Christ's, then you are Abraham's seed, and heirs according to the promise" (Gal. 3:28–29). Paul wrote to the Ephesians, "There is one body and one Spirit, just as you were called in one hope of your calling; one Lord, one faith, one baptism; one God and Father of all, who is above all, and through all, and in you all" (Eph. 4:4–6).

> **As believers in Christ, we are all part of the same Body of Christ that encompasses the entire world. The Holy Spirit connects you to believers everywhere.**

Jesus prayed for His disciples and us on the night before His crucifixion:

I do not pray for these alone, but also for those who will believe in Me through their word; that they all may be one, as You, Father, are in Me, and I in You; that they also may be one in Us, that the world may believe that You sent Me. And the glory which You gave Me I have given them, that they may be one just as We are one: I in them, and You in Me; that they may be made perfect in one, and that the world may know that You have sent Me, and have loved them as you have loved Me. (John 17:20–23)

Jesus' prayer was that we might have a strong sense of belonging to God, and that we might have a strong sense of belonging to one another, to the extent that we have a "oneness" in belief, fellowship, communication, faith, and purpose.

Every person has a lonely moment now and then. Do I ever get lonely? Yes. But I know what to do when I'm lonely. I work on my relationship with the Lord Jesus Christ. And I reach out to call friends and invite them to come over or go someplace with me. No person needs to accept loneliness as a fact of his or her life. Nor does God desire for loneliness to be the general state of being for any person. Deep loneliness and peace cannot coexist.

Jesus always called His people to be in association with one another. He sent out His disciples two by two (Luke 10:1). He said He would be present wherever "two or three are gathered together in My name" (Matt. 18:20). He said that if "two of you agree on earth concerning anything that they ask," He would do it (Matt. 18:19).

A person who lives as an island is a person who has opted for an isolated, lonely, out-of-touch-with-others existence. No person can live that way long before deep unrest invades his heart.

Trust God to help you gain a strong sense of belonging to Him, and to provide for you a "family" of fellow believers to whom you can belong.

As you grow, then, in friendships, reach out to others. Genuinely and generously give to others. Give your time. Give words of sincere affection. Give a listening ear. Give comfort. Give encouragement. Love others with the love of the Lord flowing through you to them.

Become a loyal and faithful member of your church. Find a place where you feel you truly "belong" and nurture those who are in that community with you. Even as you bond together with other believers, reach out to those who don't believe to encourage them to join your group and be part of your warm fellowship.

Essential Belief #5:
God Has a Plan for Your Fulfillment

For real inner peace, a person needs to know that he or she is competent, able, capable, and skilled at doing something. The "something" may be a task that the world as a whole considers to be a menial chore or service. Nonetheless, if you can do that task, and you know that you do it well, you are competent!

Many years ago I had lunch with a group of people at a restaurant that is part of a popular chain. We were sitting at a table that gave us a view of the short-order cooks in the kitchen area. One of the women in the group, whom I knew to be a gourmet cook, said as she watched the cooks at work, "I love to cook and I'm a good cook, but I'll tell you one thing, I could never do what those guys do."

I said, "What do you mean?"

She said, "I could never juggle that many orders, fix that many kinds of food, hear new orders coming in from several waitresses, prepare an order all in a matter of minutes, and figure out how to keep the grill cleaned and French fries in the fryer all along the way."

There's a wonderful sense of peace that comes when you know you are capable of putting in a good performance or doing a good job. That's true if you are a concert violinist about to walk onto the stage for a performance . . . a baseball player about to step out of the dugout to the batter's box . . . a mom who is diapering a baby while keeping a watchful eye on a busy two-year-old child . . . a lawyer about to make an opening statement before a jury . . . a teacher preparing to greet a class on the first day of school . . . a surgeon about to walk into a surgical suite . . . or a short-order beginning to prepare a cheeseburger.

REJECT NAGGING SELF-DOUBTS

Those who don't feel competent have a feeling that they might be about to fail. They often say to themselves, "I don't really know how to do this and I'm about to be found out," "What if I hurt somebody because I'm just not good enough at this?" or "I shouldn't be here doing this." Those nagging self-doubts destroy inner peace.

God's desire is for every person to become skilled at using the talents and aptitudes he or she was given from birth. He also greatly desires each to use the ministry gift received at the time of their salvation. The turning of talents and gifts into skills is part of our responsibility. It sometimes takes education or the acquiring of specific knowledge in order to become competent. It sometimes takes the learning of repetitive tasks. It always takes practice. Nobody is fully competent at any activity the first time he or she tries that activity—that was true for you as a toddler learning to walk and feed yourself as much as it is true for a business intern learning to trade stocks or a young preacher about to enter the pulpit for the first time. You may be good as a rookie, but if you are honest with yourself, you'll recognize you aren't an expert the first time out in the application of any skill.

CONTINUE TO LEARN AND PRACTICE

God's desire is that we continue to develop in our talents, aptitudes, and ministry gifts every day of our lives. We should never stop practicing or stop learning, no matter how experienced and skilled we may become. I'm told that the truly great concert pianists still practice playing scales on a routine basis. Top athletes still work out and practice "basic drills" during training camps and warm-up sessions, no matter how many years they've been in the professional ranks.

My favorite hobby is taking photographs, developing the film, and printing photos in my darkroom. I've taken literally tens of thousands of photographs in my life. I've also attended seminars and availed myself of expert instruction on a number of occasions. I routinely read magazines and instructional materials that describe new darkroom techniques or tell about new camera and film products. I'm a much better photographer than I was thirty years ago, but I also firmly believe that I'm not as good a photographer as I'm going to be ten years from now! I intend to keep learning and keep improving every year for the rest of my life.

God will not lead you to "become" something without aiding you to become the "best" you can possibly be in that area. He will not give you a talent and then fail to give you opportunities for discovering, using, developing, practicing, and perfecting it.

TRUST GOD TO HELP YOU LEARN AND GROW

Please do not misunderstand me on this matter of competency—there's nothing wrong with feeling a certain amount of incompetence or inadequacy. Incompetence and inadequacy are two different things:

- Incompetence says, "I can't do this because I'm lacking something."
- Inadequacy says, "I can't do this in my own strength."

The apostle Paul wrote, "Not that we are sufficient of ourselves to think of anything as being from ourselves, but our sufficiency is from God" (2 Cor. 3:5).

The very fact that you are capable of continuing to learn and develop tells you that you will never be fully competent at anything. Each of us will always have plenty of room for growth, and that's part of God's design for us. We also will never be fully adequate because we will always have a need for God to do in us, for us, and through us what He alone can do. God is the author and finisher of our lives; not only of our faith, but of all aspects of the potential He has built into us.

> **The very fact that you are capable of continuing to learn and develop tells you that you will never be fully competent at anything. Each of us will always have plenty of room for growth, and that's part of God's design for us.**

As a pastor, I know that it is the Lord who "completes" what I preach—I often receive reports of how He has caused a person to hear something I have preached with greater emphasis or greater impact than I put into the sermon. The Lord has a way of personalizing His Word, including the preached Word, for every person who hears it. He does this so the person will apply the message to his or her own heart and life, and respond in the way the Father desires. Truly, the sufficiency of any sermon lies in what God does with it after it leaves a preacher's lips.

The same thing is true for your job, no matter what that job is. You can teach to the best of your ability, but it is the Lord who will complete the learning process in a student's mind and heart. You can perform a surgical procedure to the best of your ability, but it is the Lord who will complete the healing process in a patient's life. You can plant seeds and then water, fertilize, and cultivate a field, but it is the Lord who turns seeds into a harvest.

Don't ever lock yourself into saying, "I can't, I can't, I can't," when you feel less than fully competent. Instead say, "By the grace of God and with the help of God, I can do this. The Lord is my sufficiency. He is living inside me, and He will make me adequate for whatever task He calls me to accomplish. He will give me the insights, knowledge, direction, strength, energy, vitality, focus, associations, contacts, and all other things that are necessary!"

Anytime you feel inadequate, go to God and say, "I feel inadequate. I'm trusting You to be my adequacy."

If you feel ignorant, trust God to be your source of wisdom.

If you feel weak or exhausted, trust God to be your strength.

If you feel yourself totally without adequate resources, trust God to provide what you need.

The apostle Paul said, "I can do all things through Christ who strengthens me" (Phil. 4:13). He also wrote how the Lord had spoken to him and said, "My grace is sufficient for you, for My strength is made perfect in weakness." Paul's response was, "Therefore most gladly I will rather boast in my infirmities, that the power of Christ may rest upon me . . . For when I am weak, then I am strong" (2 Cor. 12:9–10).

Paul knew that in every area where he was weak, Christ would more than make up for his weakness, and the result would be far more strength than he could ever have apart from Christ. The same is true for you and me. When we rely on Jesus Christ to be our sufficiency, He steps in and makes us "more" than anything we could ever be in our own strength, intellect, or ability. If we are willing to trust Him and rely upon Him, He will take what we offer— doing our best and giving our best—and enhance it with His own presence, power, wisdom, and creative Spirit. He will produce more than would otherwise be physically, naturally, or materially possible.

All of us face things in our lives that we have never done before. Any new venture—whether it is going away to college, getting married, having a baby, starting a new job or launching a business, changing a career, embarking on an outreach ministry— will challenge your competence. If you wait until you "get it all together" before you try something you've never done before, you'll never step out to try anything. It takes faith to start something—and part of our expression of faith is our saying within ourselves, "I may be inadequate in myself . . . but with Christ dwelling in me and executing His will, plan, and purpose in me, I am adequate!"

A person who feels he or she is a "failure" does not have peace. A person who feels as if he is on thin ice, is in over his head, or has taken on more than he can carry, does not have peace.

Believe God when He says that He loves you. Trust Him to help you fulfill anything He leads you to undertake.

Never Discredit Your Purpose

Finally, when God reveals His purpose to you, never discount that purpose. Never say to others, "I'm just a . . ."

Every form of honest, morally sound, godly work is worthy of reward, worthy of your doing it to the best of your ability, and worthy of respect.

Why Such an Emphasis on What You Believe About God?

Why am I placing such great importance on what you believe about God and His relationship to you?

Because if you truly believe God is not sovereign . . .

If you don't believe God desires to provide fully for you—materially, physically, emotionally, spiritually . . .

If you don't believe God considers you to be worthy and lovable . . .

If you don't believe God cares about your loneliness . . .

If you don't believe God has a plan for your fulfillment and deep satisfaction . . .

You are never going to trust God to do what He wants to do for you. You are never going to trust Him to give you peace. You are never going to put yourself in a position to receive all the blessings He desires to pour out upon you.

Just as it is critically important that you not lay down your peace, it is just as critical that you pick up, embrace fully, and become firmly committed to right beliefs about God and His relationship with you.

If you are a person who holds to relative truth, if you are a person who quickly compromises your beliefs or who has no real convictions, you are not going to have deep peace. You can't have deep peace. You will always be in some kind of flux on the inside, moving from emotion to emotion and from opinion to opinion, never really reaching a place where you have "settled the matter" in your mind and heart about the most important issues of life.

Face your life today. Do you have deep tranquillity? Do you genuinely value who you are, why you are on the earth, and the traits God has given you? Do you like the person God created you to be? Do you believe God has a plan and purpose for you? Do you believe He has a "place" where you can belong and be loved?

If not, ask the Lord to help you address the inner conflict you feel. His desire is that you might experience serenity in your heart so you can truly enjoy your life, your relationships with other people, and your relationship with Him. He wants to bind up the fragmentation, connect the pieces of your life, and calm the agitation you feel within. He desires to give you peace and end the turmoil in your own heart.

∞

SIX

How Your Thought Life Affects Your Peace

A few years ago I took a photography trip to the Canadian Rockies. After a couple of days of taking photographs in this beautiful area of the world, I began to wish for a little snow. There's something wonderful about snow in the mountains— photographs of mountains, evergreen trees, rocks, and other rugged-terrain features have much more contrast and are more interesting after a snowfall, and especially so if you are shooting with black-and-white film. I went to bed one night praying for snow—not too much, of course, but "just enough."

In what seemed like the middle of the night, I awoke with a heavy weight on my chest and down my legs. My tent had collapsed. My first thought was, *Bear!* I felt certain a bear had pounced on the tent in search of a midnight snack—I didn't want it to be me!

I lay perfectly still, thankful that I was still able to breathe.

Finally, when I heard no "bear sounds" and felt no movement, I began to squirm a little and, eventually, pushed up the tent and crawled out.

Did I find evidence of a bear? No. What I found was about six inches of snow covering our campsite, including tents and all our gear. My tent had collapsed under the weight of this early-fall wet snow.

Even though I had prayed for snow, I had been surprised by it. My mind had not concluded, *It must have snowed,* when my tent collapsed. Rather, my mind had concluded, *I'm about to be eaten alive!* And my body had reacted according to my thought. If I had been thinking *snow,* I certainly would not have felt a gripping, paralyzing fear.

Most of us don't like to face this even though we know it to be true: What you think makes a huge difference in what you say and do. Your thoughts, which flow out of your basic beliefs, are like the traffic controllers of your life. They determine where you go, what activities you pursue, how you pursue them, the people you are willing to include in your life, and many other factors, all of which result in your ultimate success or failure.

The way you think about other people also becomes the way you treat other people. The way you think about situations becomes the way you respond to them. Those things you think are important become your "priorities," and in turn, your priorities determine how you plan a week, schedule a day, or map out a set of plans and goals.

CHOOSE TO CHANGE THE WAY YOU THINK

Most people aren't really what they think they are. Most people have an overly inflated, inaccurate, or overly negative impression of themselves. Our human tendency is toward pride, error, or low self-esteem, or a combination of these. Our self-perception is often very skewed by self-justification, selfish desires, or the influence of others around us.

Many people have a thought life that is a little like concrete—it's all mixed up and extremely rigid! They have acquired a mishmash of both good and bad thinking. They have confused that with their fleshly desires and have hardened their hearts to any godly change.

God's Word refers to such people as "stiff-necked" or as having a "heart of stone." They are stubbornly intent on living their lives according to their own rules and emotional impulses, with very little regard for the ways in which they hurt others, and virtually no regard for what God desires.

No, most of us are not what we think we are. Our thinking is marred and needs to be changed.

How do I know this to be true? Not only by the many people with whom I have had contact through the years, but also from God's Word. The Bible calls us to a "renewal" of our minds. That means change. That means trading in our old perceptions, old opinions, old ideas, old beliefs, and old self-centered attitudes on a new set of perceptions, opinions, ideas, beliefs, and attitudes that God develops in us. Most mature believers will tell you that these godly responses are nurtured by regular reading of Scripture and meditating on what one reads in the Bible. Christ's followers are urged to avoid being "conformed to this world, but be transformed by the renewing of your mind, that you may prove what is that good and acceptable and perfect will of God" (Rom. 12:2).

Out of a renewal of our thinking comes a change in our speech patterns and our behavior. As our speech and behavior become renewed, our relationships with others become renewed. As our relationships with others become renewed, our immediate world becomes renewed. It all begins in the mind—with what we choose to think about and what we choose to dwell upon.

SEVEN CATEGORIES OF PEACE-DESTROYING THOUGHTS

There are seven categories of thoughts that will do great damage to your peace:

1. SINFUL THOUGHTS

These thoughts include lustful desires for power, money, prestige, or sex outside marriage. Lust and peace cannot inhabit the same heart. Lust is a controlling desire—lust both entices and compels a person to do what is contrary to God's commandments. Sinful thoughts also include anger, resentment, envy, bitterness, hatred, hostility, controlling fears, and thoughts of revenge. These, too, are contrary to God's Word.

The Bible describes these as "wicked" thoughts. They drive a person away from God, rather than toward God.

> **Lust and peace cannot inhabit the same heart.**

The angry person is not a peaceful person.
The bitter or resentful person is not a peaceful person.
The person consumed with sexual lust is not at peace. Neither

is the person consumed with a lust for material goods, status, or power over others.

The person with hate and vengeance is not a peaceful person. Neither is a person consumed with envy or a covetous spirit. Neither is a person with strong prejudices and arguments that they simply refuse to give up, even in the light of an abundance of contrary evidence.

The person filled with a controlling fear is not at peace.

The devil's deception is that you can harbor sinful thoughts and attitudes, and engage in sinful behaviors, and still have peace. God's truth is that unless you confront these thought patterns in your life, confess them to God to be forgiven, and then begin to trust the Holy Spirit to help you turn toward positive, godly patterns of thinking—you cannot know peace.

2. SELF-LIMITING THOUGHTS

I have heard so many people say through the years, "I know God has called me, but I just can't be in ministry" or "I know God has this for me, but I'm not qualified or worthy to receive it" or "I know people don't like me" or "I know people from my background just don't make it in life."

Self-limiting thoughts are rooted in deep feelings of rejection, lack of worth, or lack of love. Many of these feelings originate in early childhood.

Parents, you can set your child on a path toward a lifetime of anxiety and inner turmoil if you convey that your child is unwanted, unloved, untalented, or without merit or ability.

The more you put yourself down, the more you deny God's power to raise you up. The more you diminish the gifts and talents

God has built into your life, the less likely you will be to seek to develop those gifts and talents.

The self-limiting person is restless, frustrated, and anxious inside—there's a part of his or her potential that is longing to be used, but self-limiting thinking is keeping that potential bottled up with no outlet. The result is no peace.

3. ERRONEOUS THOUGHTS

Sometimes we think "incorrectly" because we are ignorant. We simply don't know the motivation of a person, the truth about a circumstance, or the facts of a situation.

Most people tend to think the worst about other people, rather than think the best. If you think a person is bad, untrustworthy, or unworthy of your time or attention, without value in God's eyes, dishonest, hurtful, or evil—you aren't going to want to be in relationship with that person. You aren't going to be willing to get close or be vulnerable to him. You are going to have a little fear or anxiety toward him. Those feelings are incompatible with peace.

Sometimes we are correct in our assessment of other people— but sometimes we are wrong. What we perceive to be a haughty, indifferent attitude may actually be a sense of reserve or quiet evaluation in the other person. Often what we perceive to be pride is actually confidence. What we perceive to be a manipulative attitude is actually a desire to help.

It is important to make certain that our perceptions are accurate. Evaluate why you hold to the opinions about another person. Do your opinions remain constant over time, in a variety of circumstances and situations, and true in relationships other than the one you have with that person?

Another major error a person makes is to think he is isolated and alone. The truth is that nobody is really alone. God has someone He desires to provide to you as a friend, mentor, counselor, minister, teacher, spouse, or neighbor. The person who says, "I'm alone," is a person who perceives that nobody is giving to him. The antidote for loneliness is always to start giving to others! When you turn yourself inside out from being an "I must receive" person to an "I must give" person, you will find yourself in relationships with people, and you will not be alone!

There is somebody who needs something you have to give. It may be your listening ear, your wise counsel, your practical help, your intercessory prayers, or perhaps just your presence next to him or her. Find an outlet for giving and you will not be alone. You are likely to find that the somebody God has destined to be your friend is a person you will meet as you give. That person will either be a recipient of your giving or a co-giver alongside you.

> **The truth is that nobody is really alone. God has someone He desires to provide to you as a friend, mentor, counselor, minister, teacher, spouse, or neighbor.**

Errors in our thinking about God. Unfortunately, many people tend to think the worst about God, rather than to believe the best about Him! Previously in this book, I have mentioned the serious mistakes some people make in their perceptions about God, but I want to reemphasize the folly of this thinking.

Through the years I have repeatedly heard God blamed for a tragedy, catastrophe, or the death of a beloved family member or friend. God doesn't send tragedies into a person's life. That's the work of the enemy of our souls. The person who blames God for things that have gone wrong in his or her life—including various injustices, abuses, or prejudices held against him or her—is a person who is unwilling to trust God. The truth is that trusting God is at the heart of peace.

Think for a moment about a young child or baby lying peacefully asleep or quietly and calmly awake in the mother's arms. That baby has a total sense of trust that the mother's arms are secure. Her trust allows her to rest in peace.

If a child, however, is in the arms of a stranger—someone she doesn't know and therefore doesn't trust—that child will be agitated, fussy, nervous, and is likely to begin crying in anxiety. She doesn't have peace.

The same principle applies to us. When we have any opinion about God that diminishes our trust of Him, we are going to feel anxious.

Errors in our thinking about God's Word. Many people have incorrect concepts about the Bible. They believe it isn't accurate, it isn't the Word of God, it isn't valid for today's world, or that it doesn't relate to their everyday lives. They are wrong on all counts. The person who doesn't trust the accuracy and truthfulness of God's Word is a person who has no foundation for finding, receiving, or accepting God's offer of peace. Without the Bible there is no basis on which to trust God, receive God's forgiveness, or know with certainty what is right and wrong. There's no foundation for a genuine understanding about how to develop an ongoing relationship with God or a peaceful relationship with others outside His word.

Errors in our thinking about salvation. Three of the biggest errors that I hear about salvation are these:

- *I've sinned too much to be saved.* The Lord is frequently portrayed in the Scriptures as being "long-suffering" toward us—which means He is patient. He is portrayed as being filled with mercy toward us, which means He stands ready to forgive the moment we turn to Him to confess our sins and receive His mercy. From the foundation of time, His desire has always been that we receive Jesus as our Savior and live with Him forever.

- *I've committed the unpardonable sin.* The very fact that you are questioning if you have committed the unpardonable sin means that you haven't. Those who commit the unpardonable sin are those who have rejected God to the point that they have absolutely no desire to know God or have a relationship with Him. They have completely cut themselves off from any awareness of God and they are void of conscience. I seriously doubt that you have done this if you are reading this book!

- *I'm saved right now, but I'm not sure my salvation will last.* The Bible tells us that those who receive Jesus as their Savior are born anew in their spirit. What is "birthed" by the Holy Spirit can never be "unbirthed" by Him. The Holy Spirit "seals" us as God's children forever. There's nothing we or anybody else can do to "unseal" what God has sealed.

You may vacillate in your spiritual disciplines. You may walk away from God and come to a place where you no longer experience close fellowship with Him. You may reject the convicting nudges of the Holy Spirit in pursuit of your own sinful desires. You may miss out on many opportunities and blessings that God desires to give you. You may fail to pursue God's call on your life and miss out on many of the eternal rewards God had planned for you. But I believe you cannot "undo" your salvation.

Those who genuinely receive Jesus Christ as their Savior will want to know Him better, obey Him, follow Him, and continue to mature in their faith. Rather than question if you are saved forever, you perhaps should ask yourself, "Have I ever truly surrendered my whole life to the Lord?" If you have, then you are Christ's own forever. The conviction you feel in your heart is not the conviction to accept Christ as Savior, but rather, a conviction to return to Christ and follow Him more closely as your Lord.

These three main errors regarding your salvation can destroy your peace. They create a shaky foundation for your faith. Peace is something that comes as a by-product of believing what is true about God and His forgiveness of your sin.

Errors in thinking about the church. If you begin to believe that you do not need to be in fellowship with other believers, you will isolate yourself from genuine friendship and opportunities to give your ministry gifts and receive the ministry gifts of others. Then you very likely will feel stifled, lonely, or disconnected spiritually. You may feel rejected, unloved, unwanted, or estranged. None of these emotions are compatible with deep inner peace. They are the result of an error in thinking that a person can "go it alone" spiritually. God set His people into a "body" of fellowship so that we each might minister to other people and receive benefit from other believers (Rom. 12:3–13; 1 Cor. 12:4–11; Heb. 10:25).

4. Unrealistic Thoughts

Suppose I said to you, "I'm going to resign from being a pastor, and within five years I'm going to be a rocket scientist." That would be one of the most unrealistic statements I could ever make!

Anytime people set goals for their lives that require great striving, intense frustration, repeated failures, and manipulation of others—that is an unrealistic goal. It is not within the realm of their God-given talents and abilities. It is beyond God's plan and purpose for their life.

Now, I'm not saying that the achievement of goals doesn't require effort, education, training, or the development of skills. Those factors are always involved in the attainment of any goal that is worthy. God doesn't give us talents and abilities that are fully developed. He requires that we sharpen them and mature in their use.

It is another thing entirely to set yourself to becoming an opera singer when you can't carry a tune in a bucket, to pursue a career as a gymnast when you are a thirty-year-old six-foot-tall woman with a heavy bone structure, to desire to be the curator of an art gallery when you are color-blind, to pursue a career as an accountant when math has always been a difficult subject, to seek to become a nurse when you don't really like being around sick people, and on and on I could go. To set an unrealistic goal for yourself is to invite anxiety, frustration, and inner turmoil.

Any idea you pursue that is contrary to God's purpose for your life, His commands in the Bible, or the plan of salvation is an idea that is not rooted in reality. It is an idea that has a built-in flaw. It is an idea that will cause you great inner agitation, not peace.

God will not lead you into unrealistic thinking.

"Seemingly impossible" and "unrealistic" are not the same. "But," you may say, "the Lord seems to be nudging me toward a goal that seems impossible to me." I didn't say the Lord wouldn't challenge you to do what seems impossible to you. I said He wouldn't lead you into something that was unrealistic.

The "impossible goals" that the Lord lays before us are goals that are in keeping with the talents and abilities He has given us. They are things that we cannot achieve apart from the use of our faith. There is a dimension to these goals that is God's realm. Only He can cause all the pieces to fall into place. Only He can cause the seeds of time, effort, and skill associated with the goal to come to full fruition.

A number of years ago I heard about a man who had two dreams. One was the dream of purchasing a fairly large acreage of farmland. There was only one problem with this idea. There wasn't sufficient water to produce crops that would have high enough cash value to make the payments on the land. The other dream was one of giving a million dollars, over a twenty-year period, toward helping to spread God's message and ministry in the world.

Were these unrealistic goals? No. This man already farmed several hundred acres. He had grown up in a farming family and he had been farming all his life. He knew what it took to make land productive. He also was a faithful giver of his tithes and offerings. He was already giving about twenty thousand dollars a year to the church. Plus, he had a very strong belief that God was going to provide a way of bringing water to the land he had in mind, and he had already consulted engineers and geologists about various irrigation plans.

This man felt so strongly he was to purchase the land that he made a down payment on it. And within a matter of weeks after he took that step, word was released that the government was going to construct a multibillion-dollar water project. A major canal was going to be constructed adjacent to the property this man had just purchased!

Overnight, the value of this land quadrupled. He sold a couple hundred acres at a great profit, which gave him the money to further develop the remaining land and plant in it high-cash crops. He reached his goal of giving away a million dollars to missionary causes in twelve years, not twenty!

Was this man's dream unrealistic? No. It was in keeping with his abilities, his desires, his experience, and the area in which he already lived. Was his dream "impossible"? In the minds of many, yes. Those who looked only at the present reality of the land could not imagine how it might produce viable high-dollar crops one day. A great deal of faith and waiting on God for His timing was required. The goal was not impossible; it only seemed impossible at that time.

5. REBELLIOUS THOUGHTS

Those who engage in rebellious thinking are those who say, "I know what God's Word says, but I'm going to do what I want to do anyway." I can remember sitting and talking to a man on his front porch. He told me what he was going to do and I said, "You'll never have any peace if you do that. That's a violation of the law of God."

He looked me right in the eye and said, "I know it is. But I'm going to do it anyway because that's what I want."

I said, "Please don't. You'll be making a terrible mistake."

"Maybe so," he said, "but it will be my mistake."

Things turned out exactly as he wanted—and as I had predicted. The choices he made created a disaster in his life, and in the lives of all who were innocently involved.

"All-too-natural" rebellion. There's a form of rebellion that is rooted in this choice: "It seemed natural to me."

Anytime you have an idea that just "feels right" in your emotions or "feels like the natural human thing to do," stop yourself. Reevaluate what you are thinking about doing. Weigh it against the commands of God. What we "feel" like doing in the moment is often not what is right to do.

> **Anytime you have an idea that just "feels right" in your emotions or "feels like the natural human thing to do," stop yourself.**

Most of the impulses of the natural man are rooted in selfish desires—greed, lust, a craving for power or control. When we operate out of that "natural" approach to life, we nearly always end up in a mess. We are operating apart from God's plan, and He cannot impart peace or blessing on a plan that is contrary to His will.

"Hesitation" rebellion. There's a second form of rebellion that I call "hesitation rebellion." A person may know with great clarity and confirmation what God wants her to do, but she waits, saying, "I'm thinking about it." Her hesitation may be rooted in fear or self-doubt. It may be based in a lack of faith; a perceived lack of

energy, strength, or resources required for the task; or in simple laziness. Sometimes a person just doesn't want to make the extra effort that will be required to move out of his comfort zone and into a new challenge. The end result is rebellion—it is saying, "I know best about God's timing. I'll do what God says when I want to do it, not when He wants me to do it."

"Exception" rebellion. A third form of rebellion is saying to God, "I surrender all of my life to You, except this area." The area that remains unsurrendered is an expression of rebellion.

Every one of us has the potential for being rebellious in our thinking. Never assume you are too mature in your faith or too wise to fall into rebellion. Ask the Lord to reveal to you any area in which you remain stubbornly committed to doing things your way, even though you know your way is contrary to God's way, God's timing, or God's desire to have all of your life.

There is no compensation for a rebellious attitude or mind-set. No amount of good works or financial giving can make up for the fact that you are in disobedience. What you will reap from this attitude is a continual churning inside. There is no peace for the rebellious heart.

6. OBSESSIVE THOUGHTS

Obsessive thoughts are thoughts that harass and dominate a person, dividing his mind and fracturing his thinking. The person who has an obsession cannot focus on anything other than his or her attainment of the desired object or goal.

The obsessive thought may be a thought of vengeance—a person is so intent on "getting even" or about a particular matter that all other normal activities and responsibilities of life fall by the wayside. The person's conversation and actions all orbit around the central idea of vengeance. Every waking thought is diverted to ways in which to retaliate and cause pain or disruption to the life of the person he believes has offended him.

Many people are obsessed with the way they look—what they are wearing, what they own, what they drive, where they live. Others are obsessed with thinking that they must be seen in public with "the right people."

Part of what makes a thought obsessive is its quality of control or possession. Obsessive thoughts are rooted in the attitude "I've got to have this. I've got to possess this, control this, own this, experience this." When that type of thinking takes over a person's mind, there is no peace.

Obsessive thoughts always lead people to make something or someone a greater priority than their allegiance to God. A simultaneous commitment to God and an ongoing experience of obsessive thinking do not go together.

"But what," you may say, "about the person who continually thinks about work?" Workaholics can be obsessive, often to the neglect of their spiritual lives and their families. Obsessions do not produce balance in life; they do not produce eternal fruit. If you find that thoughts of work crowd out all other thoughts, be concerned. For example, if you find yourself constantly and only thinking about work such that you cannot enjoy a vacation, you're into obsessive thinking. Ask God to help you regain your primary focus on Him.

You will not have peace in your life as long as you allow your-self to be consumed by an obsession.

7. ENSLAVED THOUGHTS

Enslaved thinking is one step beyond obsessive thinking. A per-son moves into enslaved thinking when he wants to think about something else and can't.

Most addicts are victims of enslaved thinking. They cannot escape thinking about the thing to which they are addicted. The alcoholic is always planning the next drink. The drug user is always thinking about the next fix. Thoughts related to the addiction fill every waking hour.

People who engage habitually in sin can have enslaved think-ing. For example, a person who habitually steals may feel driven to think in an enslaved way about his next robbery—his thoughts continually turn toward what he can steal and from whom. The thoughts of those who are into pornography or aberrant sexual behaviors are enslaved—their entire focus in life is on sex.

Obsessive thoughts generally take the tack, "I've got to have this." Enslaved thoughts are in the pattern "I can't live without this."

NIGHTMARES AND OUR THOUGHT LIVES

All the above types of thinking come during our waking hours. Many people also suffer from nightmares, a type of concious "thinking" that comes out of our subconscious minds. Bad dreams can be ones marked by sinful, impure, vengeful, hateful, or oth-erwise negative behavior. Bad dreams that are repeated may very well be a sign of subconscious obsession or enslaved thinking.

I'm not talking about the occasional "bad dream" that may come as the result of eating heavily spiced foods too late in the evening. I'm talking about recurring nightmares—ones that cause you to wake up in a cold sweat or with great fear. I'm talking about dreams that you can't seem to stop thinking about all through the next day. I'm talking about dreams that seem to "haunt" you, and dreams that are extremely vivid in negative imagery or language.

You may find that it takes serious fasting and prayer for you to be free of such nightmares. The same goes for obsessive thinking and enslaved thinking. You need to rebuild new patterns of thinking in your life based on God's word. The Holy Spirit will renew your mind to think in a new way. Your old fears and worries will be miraculously transformed by the power of God.

Several years ago a woman told me about her experience with nightmares. Her bad dreams came in the aftermath of being divorced by her husband, who had rejected her so he could pursue a homosexual relationship. Several times a week, this woman dreamed about her former husband coming to her, shouting highly critical comments at her until, in her dream, she was reduced to tears. Then he would turn and rush away, leaving her alone in her sorrow. She often awoke from these nightmares to find she had been "crying in her sleep," her face wet with tears. She felt sorrow, anger, hurt, and rejection all through the day after a night in which she had one of these terrible haunting dreams. She had no peace.

"During daylight hours, if I thought about the rejection and pain of my divorce, I could handle it," she said. "I'd pray and feel my peace return. But no amount of prayer on my part seemed to keep me from having these nightmares."

Then one day a friend of this woman came over early in the morning to find her still in deep sorrow and with a tearstained face. She admitted to her friend that she had been struggling with horrible nightmares for several weeks and she described the nightmares to her friend. This friend, a godly woman, immediately said, "Let's pray." In her prayer, the friend asked the Holy Spirit to deliver the woman from her enemy, heal her subconscious mind, and restore to her the peace of the Lord.

The woman who had been experiencing the nightmares told me, "I never had another nightmare after that."

You may benefit greatly from praying with a godly, Bible-believing friend about your bad patterns of thinking. Or you may need to seek out a Christian counselor or pastor who can offer a prayer of deliverance with you.

Don't just let a pattern of nightmares continue. You won't have peace until that pattern is broken. Recognize that if you are continually troubled in your sleep, God may be trying to call your attention to a particular matter. Ask Him, "Are You trying to show me something? Is there something I should know or do to be at peace in my mind?" God specifically answers this type of sincere prayer.

Don't just let a pattern of nightmares continue. You won't have peace until that pattern is broken. Recognize that if you are continually troubled in your sleep, God may be trying to call your attention to a particular matter.

PATTERNS OF BAD THINKING

A man once heard me explain this list of unproductive thoughts and said, "I have thoughts in every one of these categories!" He was utterly dismayed.

Most of us do fall into unproductive thinking from time to time. The key is not to make this unproductive thinking a pattern or a habit. Unproductive thoughts do not need to become unproductive patterns of thinking.

If you find yourself thinking the same thoughts again and again, you have developed a pattern of thinking. If you find that your thoughts seem to go round and round and never reach an end point, you have developed a pattern of thinking.

How can you turn loose of these thought patterns? It's a matter of yielding to the Lord the key to your will. It is saying to the Lord, "I can't stop thinking in this way that I know is contrary to Your Word and Your plan for my life. Help me!" Then willfully choose to think about something that is in keeping with God's Word and His plan for your life.

You may be asking, *But how can I continuously think only about godly things?*

You can't. You'd have to shut your eyes and ears and live in a vacuum not to respond with at least a passing thought to the ungodly perceptions, impressions, and words that are continually coming at you.

But here's what you can do. You can refuse to allow negative impressions and images to lodge in your mind. You can refuse to dwell upon them, rehearse them, revisualize them, or embellish them in your imagination. You can refuse to pursue them, seeking "more of the same."

If criticism or unkind behavior is leveled at you, you can refuse to allow ideas about these words or deeds of others to lodge in your heart. You can quickly turn to the Lord and say, "Father, help me to forgive this person. Help me to let go of this incident. I turn this person over to You to judge and deal with him. I turn this incident over to You, trusting You to resolve this in a way that results in good for me."

If you find yourself tossing and turning all night because of something you have heard or witnessed, turn to the Lord and say, "Father, wipe this from my mind and heart. Free me from this negative image or idea. Drive the enemy far from me and restore to me Your peace."

You Have the Power to Choose

You have the control mechanism for determining what you will think. Every person has the ability to say, "I will think about something else" and then refocus the mind on a new topic, task, or problem to solve. Every person has the ability to say, "I choose to trust God," or conclude, "I choose to be overwhelmed."

Furthermore, any child of God who takes a willful stand against thought patterns that clearly are harmful is going to be provided a way of escape from that circumstance. God will help you focus your mind on something other than your problem or bad thought pattern if you will make the initial step in that direction. Some people, because their thought processes are so unhealthy and so mired in ungodly channels, may need godly and wise counsel from a professional—a pastor or counselor. Please recognize it is never a sign of weakness or shame to ask for help from others who have the skill and experience to give you assistance in a time of need.

GUARDING OUR MINDS . . . AND OUR PEACE

Do you recall our previous reference to the aged apostle Paul sitting in chains in the prison while he wrote a letter to his friends at Philippi? He wrote:

> Be anxious for nothing, but in everything by prayer and supplication, with thanksgiving, let your requests be made known to God; and the peace of God, which surpasses all understanding, will guard your hearts and minds through Christ Jesus. (Phil. 4:6–7)

He told them that prayers offered to God with faith and thanksgiving would assure them of inner peace—no matter what trials they faced. Essentially he was saying they could make a choice—to involve God in their lives through prayer and acts of faith or they could go it alone. He also wrote to them the following:

> Finally, brethren, whatever things are true, whatever things are noble, whatever things are just, whatever things are pure, whatever things are lovely, whatever things are of good report, if there is any virtue and if there is anything praiseworthy—meditate on these things . . . and the God of peace will be with you. (Phil. 4:8–9)

This is a tremendous summary of our discussion in this chapter. We are told to focus our thinking on what is true, noble, virtuous, lovely, pure, and praiseworthy. Not only are we urged to think about such things, we are told to meditate on them.

To meditate means to fill one's mind so that the mind is constantly rehearsing, repeating, or restating what is good. To meditate is not to give a passing thought to something. To the contrary—it is to ponder something deeply, to analyze it, consider it thoroughly, and seek to fully understand it.

A word in Hebrew that is closely associated with meditation is the word we know in English as "muttering." Righteous Jews in ancient times were often heard "muttering" the Scriptures to themselves. That's the way they memorized God's Word. Few people had access to written scrolls of the Scriptures. Rather, they would hear the Word of God read in their prayer times and worship services and they would commit what they heard to memory, verbally repeating it over and over in their minds.

Let me assure you, if you set yourself to committing large sections of Scripture to memory, you are going to find your thinking is changed in the process. You simply cannot think about God's Word and think about something negative at the same time.

Meditating on the good things of life means that your mind is dominated by, permeated by, totally captivated by, and fully occupied by good ideas, concepts, and insights.

What does this mean to us in a practical sense? When we choose to think about those things that inspire us, encourage us, teach us, and build us up emotionally, we find that we want to follow God's will and we will desire to remain faithful to Him.

When we choose to think about the majesty and glory of God, we rely upon Him with increasing faith and trust.

Ultimately, the truth resides in God alone. The noblest thoughts you can produce are thoughts about God. Ultimately, it is the Lord who embodies the highest standards of justice. The Lord alone is absolutely pure and good. Those things that are of God are the things that are the loveliest, most virtuous, and most praiseworthy.

Think about how God has been faithful to you in giving you so many good things—far more good things than you can number!

Think about the plans and purposes God has for you throughout all eternity. Think about the heavenly home He is preparing for you.

You can never fully exhaust your ability to think about the goodness and greatness of God. You can never reach the end of your praise to Him.

Choose to respond to life the way Jesus responded.

Guard your prayer life.

Guard your thought life.

Seek God and all that is godly.

God's Word promises that when you fill your mind with what is virtuous and praiseworthy, "the God of peace will be with you" (Phil. 4:9).

SEVEN

LIVING WITHOUT REGRET

I remember slowly hanging up the phone and then saying as I sighed deeply, "Well, it's happened."

The voice on the other end of the phone was an attorney, notifying me that my wife had filed for divorce.

I had lived with threats of divorce for many years; my wife had moved out of our home the weekend before. And yet even so, I was stunned by the news I was given.

Over the next several days, many different emotions and thoughts tumbled through my heart and mind. I didn't want a divorce. I didn't know exactly how to proceed to keep a divorce from happening. I didn't know who to tell, or how I should tell them. I knew eventually I would need to tell the entire congregation of the church I pastored, and I had no guarantee about how the board or the people would respond. The only certainty was the pressure of preparing for and delivering next Sunday's sermon.

Even as my mind raced a million miles a second, I knew with absolute certainty deep within my heart these truths:

- God was not surprised by this action taken by my wife.

- God was in control of my life—He had allowed this to happen for His purposes and as part of His plan for me.

- God had promised in His Word never to leave me nor forsake me—He had promised He would be right by my side every step of the way—and therefore, all things would ultimately be for my eternal benefit if I would only continue to trust Him fully.

The immediate facts of the situation created turmoil. The unchanging truth about God created peace.

Almost eight years after that attorney's phone call in June of 1993, the divorce my wife sought was legally granted to her.

People have said to me in the years since . . .

"Surely you must regret the loss of your marriage."

"Surely you must regret that you failed in your fight to save your marriage."

"Surely you must regret that all your overtures toward reconciliation didn't work."

My outward response has been mostly silence. My real, inward response to such comments is, *Saddened, yes; regret, no.*

Yes, I am saddened that my marriage ended in divorce.

No, I do not live with an abiding sense of regret.

Why not?

Because regret is rooted in unresolved guilt. I knew I had peace with God, and regret and guilt are therefore not a part of my life.

FIVE VITAL QUESTIONS TO ASK YOURSELF ABOUT REGRET

Any person who is feeling regret over his or her past needs to ask these five very important questions:

QUESTION #1: WAS THERE SOMETHING MORE I COULD HAVE DONE?

In any situation, there is usually a mix of things that a person can and can't do. If another person is involved in a situation, that mix can be very complicated.

One of the challenges we each face regarding regret is a sorting out of what was within the boundaries of our responsibility, power, ability, or decision-making choice. Some things are simply beyond our control, and those are things we should not feel guilty about. Regret is not something that pertains to what others do or the responsibility others have. Regret pertains only to what we personally can control, influence, or choose.

> **Regret is not something that pertains to what others do or the responsibility others have. Regret pertains only to what we personally can control, influence, or choose.**

If you have thoughts of *I should have . . . I ought to have . . .* or *I wish I had . . .* you are living with regret. The question you need to ask first is really this one: *Could I have?*

I feel sad at times that I didn't have a father growing up. My natural father died when I was only nine months old. My mother married a man when I was about nine years old, but he was never a "father" to me. I can't recall any kind word he ever spoke to me or any material thing he ever gave me. He was an emotionally abusive man. He was never a person I called "Dad."

I don't dwell on the fact that I didn't have a father, because I don't know what it would have been like to have a father. As a young man I wondered from time to time, *What would my life be like now if I had grown up with a godly father?* There's no way, however, I could ever answer that question. Ultimately, I don't think my life would have turned out any different than it has! Why? Because God was my Father and is my Father. I have experienced His love, His provision, His guidance, His wisdom.

Do I have regret that I didn't grow up with a father? Absolutely none. This was not a situation over which I had any control or responsibility.

There are other situations, however, over which a person does have responsibility or control and find himself saying, "Yes, there was something I could have done."

A woman told me one time in a counseling situation that she had once left her husband because he was terribly abusive to her. She returned to him a short while later and had continued to live with him. She said, "I never should have gone back to him. I regret the day I did. He stopped being physically abusive, but he never stopped being emotionally abusive. If anything, he has become increasingly abusive over the years." This woman has no peace. She has lived in a valley of regret most of her adult life.

Could she have taken steps at some point to get herself out of this dangerous situation? Yes. Could she have left him if he refused counseling or remained abusive? Yes.

There are also situations in which a person may say, "Yes, there was something I did that I should not have done."

One of my best friends died not long ago. He told me many years ago that just two weeks after he and his wife married, he found a note she had written to herself. It said, "I will never love another person except . . ." and she named another man. He was hurt beyond measure. Here was his bride, a woman he loved with all his heart, vowing to herself never to love him but to continue to love a man she wished she had married instead.

He lived in that marriage with that knowledge the rest of his life.

When his wife discovered that he knew about her note, she felt deep regret. She felt guilt over something she should not have done.

What can be done in situations such as these?

First, the person who is feeling guilty should go to God and ask for forgiveness. Own up to the mistake, the sin, the bad choice, and the poor decision.

Second, the person who is feeling guilty should seek to make amends to any person he or she has hurt. Again, admit the pain that has been inflicted and ask for forgiveness. Explore what forms of restoration or reconciliation might be possible.

The only way out of this kind of guilt and regret is forgiveness—God's forgiveness, the forgiveness of others, and the forgiveness of self.

"But what," you may be asking, "if I go to another person and he refuses to forgive me?" If you seek forgiveness from another person and he refuses to forgive you, you have done what God requires. God's forgiveness will cover your actions. Forgive yourself and move on.

What if the person you've sinned against is dead? Again,

there's nothing you can do in that case. God's forgiveness is all that is required. Accept His forgiveness and forgive yourself.

QUESTION #2: DID I FAIL TO TRUST GOD?

My mother lived with a degree of regret from the day she married my stepfather until the day she died forty-seven years later. She never had any real peace in her marriage because she had deep regrets about her decision to marry him.

The main reason my mother gave me for marrying my stepfather was that she thought I needed a male role model in my life and she also felt a need for financial support. She admitted to me one time late in her life, "I should have trusted God on both accounts."

Many bad decisions are made out of a failure to trust God.

Some say, "I acted too quickly. I should have trusted God longer."

Some say, "I didn't trust God to show me how to respond."

Some say, "I wasn't sure God was really going to provide for my need."

Regret in many people is rooted in the fact that they didn't have the courage, the strength, the fortitude, the resolve . . . and, most important, they didn't trust God to supply them with the courage, strength, fortitude, or resolve they needed.

> **If you have trusted God in a situation to the best of your ability, lay down any guilt you feel. It's false guilt.**

If you have trusted God in a situation to the best of your ability, lay down any guilt you feel. It's false guilt.

If you have not trusted God and have taken matters into your own hands, have rushed into decisions, or have acted in a way contrary to God's commandments, seek God's forgiveness.

QUESTION #3: DID I SIN?

Psalm 34:14 gives us a twofold admonition: "Depart from evil and do good; seek peace and pursue it."

Apart from mistakes and errors in timing or poor choices, many people feel regret that stems from outright sin. In these cases, a person has willfully acted in a way that violates God's commandments. There is no peace when that happens.

The only solution when you are feeling regret over sin is to go to God and confess your sin, ask for His forgiveness, and then on the basis of His Word, receive His forgiveness.

The problem many people have is that they feel regret, but they refuse to link that regret to guilt or sin. They choose instead to justify their sin or to believe that sin simply doesn't exist.

Not long ago I was counseling a young man, and he said, "You live a very sheltered life."

I responded, "You're right. I do live a sheltered life."

He said, "You're narrow-minded."

I replied, "You're right. I am."

"You don't know the people in your church," he told me. "You don't know what they're doing."

"I may not know them all personally, or know all the details of their lives, but I know this—they are seeking God in their lives or they wouldn't come Sunday after Sunday."

I went on to say, "I don't make any apology for being narrow-minded. I don't think the way the world thinks. I have spent years—yes, decades of my life—working to train my mind to think according to the Word of God. I want my thoughts and my actions to line up completely with the Bible, and that's not the way the world thinks. I have a set of standards. I put restrictions on my behavior. I have guidelines for making the choices I make. I use God's Word as my blueprint for making decisions. The world doesn't do that.

"And yes," I continued, "I'm sheltered. I'm sheltered by the Most High God. I experience the fullness of His protection, provision, and preservation. I have a deep and abiding sense that I am loved by Him, and that He is in charge of every detail of my life. I feel 'cared for' by God. Living a God-sheltered life is the best life I can imagine!

"If a broad-minded, unsheltered life is like the life you've just told me you are living—a life of confusion, oppression, and deep discontentment—then I want nothing to do with a broad-minded, unsheltered life."

You can't live free of regret and guilt, and simultaneously choose to sin. And you can't be freed from your guilt and regret until you are willing to admit that you have sinned.

The good news is that anytime we come to our heavenly Father with a sincere heart and seek His forgiveness, He grants us forgiveness!

Perhaps the most beautiful example of forgiveness is found in a story told by Jesus. Let me remind you of this story in its entirety:

A certain man had two sons. And the younger of them said to his father, "Father, give me the portion of goods that falls to me." So he divided to them his livelihood. And not many days after, the younger son gathered all together, journeyed to a far country, and there wasted his possessions with prodigal living. But when he had spent all, there arose a severe famine in that land, and he began to be in want. Then he went and joined himself to a citizen of that country, and he sent him into his fields to feed swine. And he would gladly have filled his stomach with the pods that the swine ate, and no one gave him anything.

But when he came to himself, he said, "How many of my father's hired servants have bread enough and to spare, and I perish with hunger! I will arise and go to my father, and will say to him, 'Father, I have sinned against heaven and before you, and I am no longer worthy to be called your son. Make me like one of your hired servants.'"

And he arose and came to his father. But when he was still a great way off, his father saw him and had compassion, and ran and fell on his neck and kissed him. And the son said to him, "Father, I have sinned against heaven and in your sight, and am no longer worthy to be called your son."

But the father said to his servants, "Bring out the best robe and put it on him, and put a ring on his hand and sandals on his feet. And bring the fatted calf here and kill it, and let us eat and be merry; for this my son was dead and is alive again; he was lost and is found." And they began to be merry. (Luke 15:11–24)

This boy who had rebelled reached a time when he "came to himself" and faced the reality of his life and the reality of his father's provision. He returned and surrendered his fate to the father.

When the father saw his son on the horizon, did the father say,

"There's my worthless, errant son. He looks as if he's lost it all. How can I punish him?"

No! The father ran to his son and embraced him with compassion and kisses. The son confessed his sins. And the father immediately and generously responded by restoring to his boy all the marks of "sonship" of that day—the family's "best" robe that put him in full standing as a righteous member of the household, a signet ring with which to conduct family financial affairs, and sandals that gave full freedom for him to come and go, not as a slave, but as a son about his father's business.

This prodigal boy was in no position to declare himself to be a son. He was in no position to justify himself or restore himself as an heir of the father. He was only in a position to return to his father, to confess his sins, to surrender himself, and to cease his rebellion. That, too, is our position.

But, oh, the joy of the Father when we come to Him in confession and surrender! He runs toward us. He falls upon us with compassion and mercy and the full embrace of His love.

I believe the number-one reason that Jesus told this story was to convey to us how loving our heavenly Father is. He told it so we might know how much pleasure and joy the Father has when we surrender our lives to Him so He might, in turn, bestow upon us all the blessings He has already prepared for us.

Our surrender results in the Father's forgiveness.

Our turning to Him with a totally surrendered life results in His giving to us the fullness of His life.

God's Word is very clear on this: "If we confess our sins, He is faithful and just to forgive us our sins and to cleanse us from all unrighteousness" (1 John 1:9).

If you have sinned and need God's forgiveness, I encourage you to make David's prayer your own:

> Have mercy upon me, O God,
> According to Your lovingkindness;
> According to the multitude of Your tender mercies,
> Blot out my transgressions,
> Wash me thoroughly from my iniquity,
> And cleanse me from my sin . . .
> Purge me with hyssop, and I shall be clean;
> Wash me, and I shall be whiter than snow.
> Make me hear joy and gladness . . .
> Create in me a clean heart, O God,
> And renew a steadfast spirit within me . . .
> Restore to me the joy of Your salvation,
> And uphold me by Your generous Spirit.
>
> (Ps. 51:1–2, 7–8, 10, 12)

QUESTION #4: HAVE I FORGIVEN EVERYBODY INVOLVED IN THE SITUATION I REGRET, INCLUDING MYSELF?

Perhaps the most difficult part of forgiveness for many people is forgiving themselves.

If God has forgiven you, you need to forgive yourself and go forward in your life. Don't continue to beat yourself up over something that God has forgiven.

If God has forgiven you, you also need to forgive any person or group of people whom you believe to have been associated with the sin. Do not continue to dwell on them in your mind or heart. Let them go and trust God to deal with them in His way, in His timing.

> **If God has forgiven you, you need to forgive yourself and go forward in your life. Don't continue to beat yourself up over something that God has forgiven.**

If you continue to relive and remind yourself of the sin, you will not have peace. You will bring this negative pattern of thinking and behaving into any new relationship, business venture, or circumstance that you enter in the future.

I have met a number of people through the years who have remarried almost immediately after a divorce. They received God's forgiveness, they forgave themselves, and they jumped into the next relationship that came along. Even as they did so, they continued to think about their previous spouses and all the negative things that had happened to them. They were not at peace with themselves. They had not truly forgiven themselves or their spouses. In the end, they had a very difficult time in their next relationships because they were still dealing with their guilt, shame, and the pain they had experienced.

The same is true for people who have been through business failure that involved fraud, theft, or embezzlement. In some cases, these people never think to ask for God's forgiveness for sin related to their business failures. In other cases, they continue to dwell on their sin to the point that they have a very difficult time throwing their energy and effort into a new job, new career, or new venture.

If God has forgiven you, forgive others, forgive yourself, and then open yourself up to the good opportunities that God has for you.

True, you may still have to live with consequences related to the sin. But you are never required by God to live with guilt, shame, or regret. Accept that your past mistakes may have put you into the situation you are in, but quickly acknowledge the greater truth that your past mistakes—now forgiven by God—do not need to impact the decisions or choices you will make in the future.

Remember always . . .

What God forgives, He forgives completely.

What God heals, He brings to wholeness.

What God restores, He does so without any limitations placed upon a person's potential for sharing the gospel and being a witness of God's love, mercy, and grace.

QUESTION #5: DID I DENY OR TURN AWAY FROM GOD'S REVEALED WILL FOR MY LIFE?

I heard not long ago about a woman who strongly believed that when she was twenty-three, God had called her to be a missionary in Southeast Asia. She was studying and preparing to become a missionary when she met a Christian man who was a building contractor. He had no call on his life to become a missionary. Rather, he felt called to be a businessman and to support missionaries through the earnings of his business.

This woman married the contractor, knowing full well in her heart that she was denying God's call on her life. She said, "I wanted a husband and children. He was the best, brightest, and most Christlike man I had ever met. I jumped at the chance to have a happy home."

She regretted her decision for the next twenty-five years of her life. She believed she had failed God. She had very little interest in going to church or getting involved in missions projects, in part from guilt and in part because she didn't want to face up to her feelings. Then, one day when she was forty-eight years old, she went to her husband and said, "I didn't do what God called me to do." He said to her, "I know you've been unhappy for years. I just didn't know why. I'll support you if you want to go on short-term mission trips—even as long as six months or a year."

She was elated and began to try to work with first one missionary organization and then another. None of them wanted to send her as a missionary under the auspices of their organization. Finally she took it upon herself to buy a ticket, fly to a country in Southeast Asia, and seek out a missionary there who might allow her to help in some way. She returned home four months later dejected, disillusioned, in poor health, and extremely exhausted emotionally and spiritually.

A wise pastor finally counseled her by saying to her very bluntly, "That boat sailed."

He went on to say to her, "God may have called you nearly thirty years ago to serve Him in Southeast Asia. What you need to ask yourself is this: 'What is God calling me to do right now?'"

Don't live in the regret of what "might have been" had you obeyed a specific call of God on your life in the past. There's no way of retracing those steps or regaining that opportunity.

Admit to God that you failed Him. Own up to the pride and selfish desires that were at the root of your decision to choose your way over His way. Ask God to forgive you and to lead you from this point onward. And then, as God reveals to you what He wants you to do now, obey Him.

I have met pastors who have left their positions at their churches and later regretted those decisions. Nearly always, the reasons they left their churches were personal reasons, not directives from God. They may have felt unappreciated. They may have thought that by moving they could improve their financial positions or their profiles in a church denomination. Those reasons are never good ones for leaving one church and moving to another. In the end, they nearly always find they are in churches that disappoint them just as much or more!

One of the reasons I have so few regrets in my life is that I have been afraid to get out of God's will. This is not an unhealthy or emotionally damaging kind of fear—it is a healthy fear to seek to know and do God's will. It is a healthy fear to desire to remain always in God's will and not get out of it.

"But what is God's will?" you may ask.

God's will is for you to

- keep His commandments.

- obey His directives about where to go, what to do, what to say.

- take care of the people and things that God has given to you.

- use the natural talents and abilities that God has built into your life.

- use the ministry gifts God imparted to you at the time of your salvation.

It is far easier to err on the side of leaving where you are than to err on the side of remaining. Too often, people leave situations in which they find themselves because of personal ambition, greed, or a lust for more power, fame, or recognition.

Now, I'm not talking about leaving situations that are physically or emotionally abusive. There certainly are times when it is God's wisdom for a person to leave a situation for his or her physical safety, emotional health, or spiritual well-being. Leaving a sinful situation—such as walking out of a "den of iniquity"—is always a good thing. That's not what I'm talking about. Rather, I'm talking about walking away from a ministry calling, a job, a family relationship, or a family responsibility. If a person leaves what God has clearly provided or authorized, without having a clear directive from God, there is a significantly high probability he is going to be moving out of God's will.

At the time I felt God's call to Atlanta, I didn't want to move to Atlanta. There wasn't anything in me that desired to live or minister in Atlanta. I was very happy in the church I was pastoring in Florida. I liked the people, the community, the weather, and the opportunities for ministry there. I left because God made it extremely clear that I had to move to Atlanta.

I have thought at times, *What if I hadn't moved to Atlanta?* I can hardly imagine what that life might have been like. I certainly know that I would have had no peace in Florida, or anywhere else I may have chosen to go based on my own personal desires.

There are a lot of people who live in a state of "If Ida." If I had only done this . . . if I had only said that . . . if I had only made that decision. People who live in a state of regret get stuck in the past.

Living in the past keeps a person from fulfilling what God wants him or her to do in the present! If that's the way you are living right now, I heartily recommend that you ask God to forgive you for anything you feel you did that was sinful or displeasing to Him in the past. After this, forgive yourself for what you did, and move on in your life. Choose not to dwell in the past. Choose instead to focus on the present and to set godly goals and make godly plans for your future. Ask God, "What's the next step You have for me?"

MAINTAIN A CLEAR CONSCIENCE

The best way to live without regret is to maintain a clear conscience. Let me turn each of the five questions we've just discussed into positive statements of choice:

- Choose to live in such a way that you do your best in every task and in every relationship. Give your utmost and your best effort to live in a godly manner.

- Choose to trust God in every area of your life—every decision, every choice, every opportunity He sends your way.

- Choose to obey God. Keep His commandments.

- Choose to forgive others fully and freely.

- Choose to pursue what God reveals to you as His path for you to follow.

No person can do these things in his or her limited human power. But with the Holy Spirit residing in us, we can turn from all forms of temptation to pursue the good works that God has authorized us to do.

In Acts 24:16 the apostle Paul said, "I myself always strive to have a conscience without offense toward God and men." That phrase "without offense" has also been translated as "blameless."

It is the Holy Spirit who works in us to

- prick our consciences if we are about to sin or have made a choice or decision that is going to lead us astray from God's perfect will for our lives.

- enable us to withstand and say no to a temptation.

- convict us of sin that we commit so we will turn immediately to the Lord and seek forgiveness.

- help us to pray and respond to life as we should, including prayer for others and forgiveness of others.

- show us the choices we are to make and the opportunities we are to pursue.

The Holy Spirit works in our inner minds and hearts to warn us of the dangerous temptations of the enemy, remind us of God's commandments, and make us uncomfortable with our sin, guilt, or shame to the point that we will desire to be cleansed and forgiven of our sin.

Many people live today with a raging conscience. They know they aren't living the way the Lord desires for them to live. Their consciences are boiling and churning all the time. They feel a tremendous burden of guilt that keeps them awake at night and causes them to be miserable most of their waking hours.

Many who have a guilty conscience manifest a prevailing attitude of anger. This is especially true for those people who feel deep anger churning within them even after they have accepted Jesus as their Savior. Believers who routinely act in anger are not at peace with themselves. In many cases, the cause of their rage is a guilty conscience. They know they aren't living the way God wants them to live and they are upset with Him for requiring obedience. They are dissappointed with themselves for not doing what they know to do, and upset with others whose behavior reminds them that they just aren't where they should be in their walks with the Lord.

"Things are just fantastic in my life. My conscience doesn't bother me." Some people have made statements such as this even as they told me about their activities that were clearly contrary to God's commandments. Invariably, some of these same people came to me months later and said, "Things really weren't great. The guilt inside me weighed about a thousand pounds. I couldn't sleep at night. I was miserable."

If you know you are disobeying God's commandments and His directives to you, and you don't feel your conscience bothering you, I encourage you to check the callousness of your own heart and to ask, "Why isn't my conscience bothering me?" I assure you of this: The degree to which your conscience speaks to you is in direct relationship to the amount of rebellion in your heart and the number of times you have refused to do what the Holy Spirit has prompted you to do.

If you truly want to obey God's commandments and walk

according to His principles for a godly life, your conscience is going to be tender—just a little prick from the Holy Spirit will cause you to turn away from sin. You will be quick to fall to your knees and seek God's forgiveness. If you have developed a rebellious heart and have chosen to walk according to your own self-made rules for living, your conscience is going to be calloused. It will take a giant conviction from the Holy Spirit deep in your heart for you to want to deny the lustful pleasures you desire and seek God's forgiveness for your sinful thoughts, words, or deeds.

> **The degree to which your conscience speaks to you is in direct relationship to the amount of rebellion in your heart and the number of times you have refused to do what the Holy Spirit has prompted you to do.**

The sensitivity of your conscience is a barometer of the degree to which you desire to obey God.

•THE HOLY SPIRIT DOESN'T LET GO

An unbeliever can come very close to destroying his conscience. He can become so hardened and "tuned out" to things of God that he will feel virtually no guilt associated with behaviors that are clearly contrary to God's laws.

If you are a believer in Christ Jesus, however, you cannot keep the Holy Spirit from continuing to manifest Himself in your conscience. He will not allow you to reach the point where your conscience is silent. You may muffle His convicting words to your heart. You may do your best to ignore His nudges, but you cannot completely stop His speaking to you. God does not want His people to live with a guilty conscience. He will continue to speak to you about your sin until you repent.

Many people attempt to silence their consciences by piling on more and more sin. They try to drown their consciences in alcohol, stupefy their consciences with drugs, or overwhelm their consciences with some form of illicit pleasure. Sin never silences conscience.

Confession means agreeing with God, saying, "This doesn't belong in my life, God. I admit I am sinning against You. I am in disobedience. I ask You to forgive me."

Repentance means saying to God, "I turn away from this. This sin is destroying my peace and clouding my thinking and hardening my heart. Help me to turn away from this completely and never to return to this sin."

Faith and trust in the Lord are required to carry out our repentance and to walk in a "newness" related to our habits, behaviors, or attitudes. The decision to obey God is a matter of our will. You must choose to obey, choose to confess your sin to God, choose to receive His forgiveness, choose to repent, and choose every day to ask the Lord to help you walk in repentance and obedience.

As you do this, you will live free of regret. And a life without regret is a life marked by prevailing peace.

ACTIVELY SEEK TO KNOW GOD'S PURPOSE FOR YOUR LIFE

Several times in this chapter I've mentioned the need for you to move forward with your life after you receive God's forgiveness.

To move forward means that you come to recognize and then do your best to fulfill God's purpose for your life. It means having a deep sense of purpose that protects you from foundering, wandering, and wasting time and energy. A sense of purpose is directly related to your feeling fulfilled and satisfied with how you have lived your life.

God has a purpose for your life. One of the best-known verses in the Bible is Romans 8:28, which says, "We know that all things work together for good to those who love God, to those who are the called according to His purpose." So often we focus on the first part of that verse. We take great confidence in knowing our loving heavenly Father is working all things together for our good, even those things that seem difficult or negative. As believers in Christ Jesus, we know God will act on our behalf because we "love Him."

But note the last half of that verse: "to those who are the called according to His purpose."

That phrase clearly tells us that God has a purpose for each one of us. He calls us to it. But to be one who qualifies as "those who are called" implies that we are walking in that calling, obeying God, and yielding to the direction of the Holy Spirit on a daily basis. If we are truly being obedient to God's commands and we are following His purpose for our lives to the best of our abilities, then God is fully committed to working all things together for our good—both our eternal rewards and our earthly blessings. But if we are just roaming through life on our own initiatives and at our own whims and wills, if we are not seeking God's purpose, if we are obeying God only when it suits us, if we are yielding to the directives of the Holy Spirit only when we find ourselves in a difficult situation, on what basis can we truly expect God to work things out to our eternal benefit?

I have absolutely no doubt that God will show you your purpose in life if you sincerely ask Him to reveal it to you.

I am condident He will give you the courage and power to pursue that purpose as you trust Him.

I have no doubt that He will work all things to your good as you live "according to His purpose."

And as you do these things, you will have much greater peace.

EIGHT

GIVING UP ANXIETY

When traffic on the freeway has come to a dead stop, and you've already been late to work two times this month . . .

When the news report states that the stock market has dropped five hundred points . . .

When you find drugs in your son's bedroom . . .

When you suspect that your unmarried daughter might be pregnant . . .

When the doctor says that he needs to run some more tests, and he isn't smiling as he says so . . .

The normal and natural response is anxiety. It's a feeling of being hit with something unexpected. Anxiety begins in our emotions, not our minds. It is a response to something we perceive or feel to be negative, and more specifically, something that we believe to be an attack against us.

ARE YOU DISTRACTED OR UNCERTAIN?

Anxiety is a problem we all face at one time or another. The Greek word for "anxious" in the following passage from the Sermon on

the Mount means "distracted." It is a word that refers to uncertainty. That's what anxiety produces in us. It gives us a feeling
of, *What next?* It is a feeling that the rug has been pulled out from
under us and we have no idea if we are going to fall, how hard, in
what direction, or onto what!

The word *anxious* is also translated as "worry" in the Bible. For
many people, worry has become a way of life. They live in a state
of uncertainty and worry. If that describes you, I encourage you to
read again the words of Jesus. His command to you is very plain.
In the Sermon on the Mount, Jesus said,

> Do not worry about your life, what you will eat or what you
> will drink; nor about your body, what you will put on. Is not
> life more than food and the body more than clothing? Look at
> the birds of the air, for they neither sow nor reap nor gather
> into barns; yet your heavenly Father feeds them. Are you not
> of more value than they? (Matt. 6:25–26)

This is not a suggestion. It is a command.

You may say, "But I can't help feeling anxious, I have always
been a worrier!" I've heard that from many people through the
years. My response is, "Oh, yes you can."

There's nothing about a circumstance that automatically creates anxiety. Anxiety occurs because of the way we respond to a
problem or troubling situation. Your ability to choose is part of
God's gift of free will to every human being. You can choose how
you feel. You can choose what you think about, and you can choose
how you will respond to a circumstance.

A friend of mine shared an experience she had almost a decade ago. Her elderly father, a widower, had moved into her home, and 99 percent of the time the relationship was a very positive, mutually enriching one. She recalled, however, that one day her father had been particularly cranky. Nothing had suited him, he had been verbally critical about several things, and she became irritated in return with his pessimism and negative outlook.

Then she told me, "We were getting ready to leave the house on errands and I looked up to see my father walking out the door and I thought, *That's my father. I love him. He's old and he's not going to be with me very much longer—even if he lives another ten or fifteen years, that's not very long.* I thought about how much I would miss my father when he was no longer with me, and I made a decision. It was a conscious, intentional decision. I said to myself, 'I'm going to choose to love him and enjoy being with him every day for the rest of my life or his life. We're going to live in peace.'

"I immediately began to treat my father with kindness and understanding, and within a matter of hours he had apologized for his bad mood and admitted that he really hadn't been feeling well for several days. From that day on, we had a wonderful relationship."

Yes, you can choose how you feel and how you will respond!

No situation automatically causes anxiety. It certainly isn't God's purpose for you to feel anxious—He doesn't allow situations in your life so you will have anxiety. No! God may allow a situation in your life to develop stronger faith, grow and mature, or change a bad habit or negative attitude. But God does not set you up for anxiety. He is always at work to bring you to a place where you will trust Him more, obey Him more fully, and receive more of His blessings.

God may allow a situation in your life to develop stronger faith, grow and mature, or change a bad habit or negative attitude. But God does not set you up for anxiety.

CONCERN IS NOT THE SAME AS ANXIETY

We must be careful not to confuse concern with anxiety. It is normal for a Christian to have deep concerns. Concern motivates us to intercede and to take godly actions toward meeting the needs of others. Concern, yes! Anxiety, no!

Concern is rooted in caring. We are to be concerned, for example, about our families, our health, doing a good job in our work—because we care about the well-being of our families, our personal well-being, and the success of our work. Concern involves wanting to see things done well so that God receives glory from our lives.

Some concern is also rooted in obedience. There is no place in the Scriptures where we are given license to be irresponsible. We are to live out God's commandments in our daily lives. We are to live honest and moral lives—paying our bills, telling the truth, giving a full day's effort for a full day's wage, and so forth. Living a responsible life involves a certain amount of concern rooted in a desire to be obedient to the Lord.

A concern rooted in caring or in obedience, however, is not the same as anxiety.

If your child walks into the house and has injured her ankle, you have a genuine right and responsibility to be concerned about whether her ankle is sprained or broken. Concern will lead you to action and to seek medical advice. Or consider the person who walks in to work one day, and his employer says, "We no longer need your services." Fired. Out of his office and onto the street in one day.

Concern involves wanting to see things done well so that God receives glory from our lives.

"Well, that's a good time for anxiety!" you may say.

Not according to God's Word. Concern, yes. Concern about continuing to provide for your family or yourself, concern about how and where to find another job, concern about what steps to take first . . . most definitely, yes. But to fall apart emotionally, become filled with fear, feel paralyzed, or allow strong thoughts of bankruptcy and homelessness and a bleak future to overtake one's mind . . . absolutely not! That's anxiety.

Concern is productive. It is forward-looking and positive.

Anxiety is the opposite—it is counterproductive, stuck in the present, and negative.

Concern motivates us to take action. Anxiety paralyzes us.

Concern may very well be marked by tears, expressions of sorrow and sympathy, empathy, thoughtful reflection, and quiet time for meditation. In the end, however, concern leads us to make decisions. It leads us to the point of saying, "I choose to trust in God. I choose to seek His plan and purpose in this. I choose to take the action He leads me to take."

Anxiety tends to be marked by hand-wringing, uncontrollable crying, deeply furrowed brows and slumped shoulders, sleepless nights, nervous twitches, and endless pacing. Anxiety is a treadmill that tends to keep a person in a state of fear and negativity, and without peace.

THE RESULTS OF ANXIETY

Here are seven highly negative results associated with anxiety:

1. ANXIETY DIVIDES A PERSON'S MIND

Many people live with a degree of stress that results from what I call a "divided mind." The person is working on one task, is engaged in a meeting with one group, or is involved in a conversation with one person, but in the back of that person's mind and heart, another problem or situation has center stage.

A cancer patient once said to me, "My first thought every morning and my last thought every night, and every third or fourth thought all day long is, *I have cancer.*" I feel certain that people who are fighting a major problem of any kind have times when that situation fills their minds much of the day.

A divided mind keeps a person from fully concentrating on the tasks at hand. Nagging worries or unsettling feelings distract him, causing him to live in a state of semiconfusion at all times.

A woman told me not long ago about her husband's mental illness. I asked her, "How did Bill's mental illness affect you?"

She said, "I never knew which Bill was going to be waiting for me when I got home. Would it be the sweet and loving Bill, or would it be the angry, sullen, silent Bill?"

"Did this impact your work?" I asked.

She said, "I nearly lost my job because I couldn't concentrate at work. It didn't matter if I was in a meeting or working alone at my desk, my thoughts tended to gravitate toward his situation. His refusal to get professional help or take the medicine prescribed for him, and what this was doing to our relationship. I couldn't help but dwell on what might happen to our marriage. I also wondered if his illness was something that our baby daughter might inherit biologically. I was preoccupied with thoughts about what I might do, should do, could do, and mostly by the helpless feeling that I might not be able to do anything to help.

"Since I couldn't concentrate fully, I just didn't do my best. I made careless mistakes. In the end, I was passed over for a promotion. It was then I woke up and thought, *Something has to happen here. If Bill isn't going to get help, I at least can get help for myself. I need to regain my peace.*"

2. ANXIETY LOWERS A PERSON'S PRODUCTIVITY

If a person has a divided mind, it is only logical to conclude that such a person will be less productive. He won't be able to sustain an effort and will be less likely to see any project through to a quality completion. Not only is the person less productive, but he or she is usually less efficient too. The quality of work tends to suffer.

3. ANXIETY LEADS A PERSON TO MAKE UNWISE DECISIONS

The person who cannot focus on a task is a person who generally cannot complete his required "homework" on a project, cannot perceive all facets of a problem, and cannot listen at length or with sufficient concentration to those who might give sound advice. The result is often poor decision making and problem solving. Bad choices and decisions are a setup for failure, which only leads to greater anxiety. The highly anxious person is often emotionally paralyzed to the point at which he can't make any decision, and thus, he doesn't move forward in his life. He lives in a cloud of apprehension and confusion.

4. ANXIETY DRAINS A PERSON'S ENERGY

Prolonged anxiety is exhausting. It wears out your immune system and alters certain chemical systems in your body so that you are depleted of vitamins and minerals that help you maintain a good energy level.

5. ANXIETY PRODUCES PHYSICAL AILMENTS

Scientific and medical researchers have shown through the years that anxiety produces numerous negative effects in the human body, including headaches, stomachaches, intestinal disorders, constriction of blood vessels resulting in high blood pressure and a greater likelihood of heart attacks and strokes, and biochemical disorders that put hormonal systems out of balance, which can result in multiple diseases.

In fact, some of our nation's premier medical schools are stating unequivocally that through faith and prayer, elements of anxiety, stress, and fear are positively reduced in patients with the result that many experience healing more rapidly.

6. ANXIETY ALIENATES OTHER PEOPLE

When a person is less focused or distracted, it becomes more difficult to communicate with him. Such a person often is fidgety and frustrated, quick to blame and to criticize others, and quick to become angry. Poor communication is very damaging to friendships, marriages, and parent-child relationships. The result can easily be that other people feel alienated, unwanted, or undesirable.

7. ANXIETY DEPLETES A PERSON'S JOY

The person who lives with prolonged anxiety is a person who usually feels robbed of joy. Anyone who worries continually or who continually feels overwhelmed by life is a person who has less hope and is less capable of appreciating or enjoying pleasurable moments. There always seems to be a problem lurking in the back of his mind or deep in his soul. Peace and joy cannot coexist with anxiety.

Given all these negative effects, our conclusion must be that a troubled soul is not God's plan for us! God's Word plainly says, "Do not fret—it only causes harm" (Ps. 37:8).

Peace and joy cannot coexist with anxiety.

WHAT ABOUT PANIC ATTACKS?

"Panic attack" is the term sometimes used when anxiety spins your emotions out of control. Your heart begins to race, you may begin to sweat profusely, become dizzy or light-headed, or feel as if you're falling apart.

I have had such an experience. It was sheer horror. I can understand now why some people turn to drugs when they feel the way I felt at that time. The feelings of anxiety and unrest, along with extreme fatigue, seem to deepen. I felt as though things inside me were spinning out of control and that I was coming apart at the seams. In my desperate hours I cried out to God—like a little boy calling for his daddy after a bad dream. His presence surrounded and sustained me through that difficult season.

If you don't know the Lord, what are you going to do to calm your heart and mind? If you don't know the Lord, and you face a sudden tragedy or load of stress that seems about to swamp you, what will you do to ease your emotions? It's easy to turn to drugs or alcohol or something that you hope will give you a momentary escape.

The good news is that those who truly know the Lord don't need to walk down the path that leads to chemical addiction. They can cry out to God, "Hold me! Help me! Don't let me go!" And the more they cry out to God with a sincere heart, the more God will impart to them His presence to drive away the anxiety, slow down the world that seems to be spinning out of control, and give them genuine peace.

Our loving heavenly Father holds on to us. He hears our cries. He embraces us with His everlasting arms. He holds us tightly in His comfort of us. The closer we cling to Him, the quieter our spirits become.

WHAT SHOULD WE IMMEDIATELY DO WHEN ANXIETY STRIKES?

What should we do when anxiety strikes? First and foremost, we must ask God to give us His peace and His answers. I know of a man who lives in a suburb of Atlanta. One day a couple of years ago he felt some unusual sensations in his leg. This discomfort continued, so he sought medical advice. After a series of tests, his doctor told him he had a virulent and rare form of cancer.

He was devastated by the news. An athlete in vibrant health (or so he thought), he saw his future crumbling before him. Anxiety began to grip his mind. He began to imagine all the worst possible scenarios, but thankfully, his friends gathered around him and sought to give him support and encourage his faith. They urged him to consider that God's presence and peace were available to him.

Today he is healed and is regularly helping other cancer victims as they struggle on their own journeys. He has peace, and seeks to pass it on to others. He found the secret to peace when worry and anxiety loomed across his path. How should we proceed?

Very specifically, we must ask God to deal with the problems that are filling both our conscious and subconscious minds. This is not likely something we do just once. It is something we may have to do many times throughout the day.

We must ask the Lord to help us focus all of our thoughts and energy on the immediate situation at hand.

Say to the Lord, "You are in control of this situation. I trust You to deal with this troublesome person or persons, or these circumstances. Help me to give my full attention to the task that You have put in front of me right now. Calm my heart, focus my attention, infuse my mind with Your ideas and creative solutions, and give me the strength to be diligent until this project or meeting is completed."

As Anxiety Subsides . . .

As the immediate force of an anxiety attack subsides, you need to settle this issue in your life: *Is God my loving heavenly Father at all times, always seeking my eternal best, or not?*

The key to overcoming anxiety is to get your thinking right about God. The fact is, God is sovereign. He created everything and has absolute control over every aspect of His creation. He is all-powerful, all-knowing, and ever present.

The key to overcoming anxiety is first and foremost to get your thinking right about God.

He knows absolutely everything about your situation. He knows how to produce wholeness out of brokenness. He knows how to build strength out of weakness. He knows how to heal what is sick. He knows how to bring reconciliation and love out of estrangement and hate.

Furthermore, He loves you with an unconditional, unfathomable, immeasurable love. He knows everything about you, and loves you still.

A loving heavenly Father who is in total control, all-knowing, and ever present whom you can trust. And trust is what causes anxiety to disappear.

The Choice Is Yours

You can fall into a downward spiral of anxiety. Or you can say, "Heavenly Father! I bring this to You. It's beyond my control or influence. I feel helpless in this situation, but You have the power to change it. You love me perfectly. I am trusting You to handle this in the way You see fit. I know that whatever You have planned for me is for my good. I look forward to seeing the way You choose to express Your love and wisdom and power." Friend, this is the way of peace—the road out of anxiety and worry.

❦

NINE

GETTING TO THE ROOT CAUSES
OF PROLONGED ANXIETY

A re you going to be ready?"
For years I would answer "yes" to that question preachers commonly are asked. "Yes, of course I'm going to be ready to preach a good sermon on Sunday." But deep down inside, I had self-doubts.

One of the things I felt anxious about nearly all my adult life was that I wouldn't be ready to preach on Sunday. I prayed. I studied diligently. I trusted God. But then I prayed some more and studied harder. And then . . . I prayed still more and studied still harder. I lived with the anxiety about the next sermon until the moment I stood up to preach it. Afterward, I'd begin to worry about the next Sunday's sermon. It is only in the last few years that I've had victory over that lifelong cycle of anxiety and relief.

For the most part, we are the ones who determine how long we will be anxious. Thus the need for anyone who consistently experiences anxiety attacks and an ongoing sense of being distraught and worried to have a complete physical checkup. Too often, however, we fail to deal with the issues that entangle us, and we allow worry and anxiety to settle permanently in our souls. The result is that we lose our peace.

As I experienced, if we permit negative and worry-filled thoughts to take root in our hearts, we can create a general state of anxiety. This way of thinking can become established within us and lead to negative attitudes that can last for years.

People have told me from time to time, "I'm just a worrier." Or they have told me about someone they know well, "He's always a little uptight," or "She tends to fret a lot." Some people refer to this continually anxious state as being "high-strung" or "always wound tight." If anxiety has become the norm for your life, however, you need to take a look at the reasons for that feeling. They are generally related to deep inner needs. Those needs tend to relate to one or more of the following.

THE INNER NEEDS THAT CAUSE LONG-TERM ANXIETY

1. A LACK OF SELF-WORTH

A person who feels a lack of self-worth has lost sight of his or her value to God, our heavenly Father. Again, let me remind you of what our Lord said:

> Look at the birds of the air, for they neither sow nor reap nor gather into barns; yet your heavenly Father feeds them. Are you not of more value than they? (Matt. 6:26)

I think Jesus was saying to those listening to Him that a person with low self-worth does not see his or her needs as being worth as much as the needs of the little sparrows that are continually under God's watchful eye.

So many of us do not think God is capable or desirous of meeting our needs on a daily, hourly, minute-by-minute basis. We don't see ourselves as being worthy of the care He bestows on a little bird in the yard.

I've had people say to me, "God doesn't care about my car breaking down." Yes, He does.

"God doesn't care about the leaky pipe in my bathroom." Yes, He does.

"God doesn't care whether I get a raise at work." Yes, He does.

God cares about every detail of your life, and His plan is to provide for you fully.

There are several reasons why we tend to see ourselves as being unworthy of His love, but do you remember His plan? Jesus sacrificed Himself for you and me. Nothing God could ever do would be a greater display of the truth that He considers you to be worthy of loving, nurturing, and blessing.

2. A Desire for Total Control

A second deep inner cause of anxiety is a desire to control all things to our benefit, including things over which we truly have no power. I believe this desire for power and control often springs from a lack of trust in God, who alone can control every aspect of our lives.

There are many things people do today in an effort to take charge of their lives—from taking vitamins to exercising daily, from eating five servings of fruits and vegetables to getting sufficient sleep. Now those things are beneficial, and I routinely engage in good nutritional and exercise habits. But I do so not to extend my life, but rather to give good quality to every hour I live.

A life riddled with anxiety produces the opposite of energy, vitality, increased productivity, and an abundance of life. Anxiety has been linked to numerous ailments and conditions, from heart attacks and strokes to high blood pressure, from digestive tract disorders to nervous breakdowns, from an increase in accidents at home and at work to less efficiency and less focus on any given task. You've never heard of people "worrying themselves to life"—no, the phrase we often use is that a person is "worried to death." In truth, anxiety can kill a relationship, destroy the fun of any event or experience, and detract greatly from a person's willingness to embark on new challenges and opportunities.

People worry about so many things they can never control. Your anxiety will not make a bit of difference in tomorrow's weather . . . it won't make another person love you . . . it won't allow you to relive a single second of yesterday.

Let God do what only God can do. Trust Him to act on your behalf out of His infinite love and mercy toward you.

Your anxiety will not make a bit of difference in tomorrow's weather . . . it won't make another person love you . . . it won't allow you to relive a single second of yesterday.

---

3. CONCERN FOR WHAT OTHERS THINK

We have a multibillion-dollar clothing industry in the USA, and it is built upon the premise that looking good is important.

We seek to dress well because we are concerned about how others think we look. It is true. We get anxious about our appearance and our performance in life. In other words, many of us worry about how we stack up, and that is another cause of deep inner anxiety.

We work harder with longer hours and overschedule our lives in an effort to impress others with our productivity and performance or at least to satisfy our own internal need for success.

Once in a while, we hear about some well-known executive or star in some arena of society who astonishes us all by dropping out of the fray and opting for a quieter, more serene life. Some respected politicians in my country who are practically guaranteed reelection are opting out even as I write this book. This goes against the grain of our American culture of "success at any cost" and causes some people to reevaluate their own priorities—which is a good thing. It allows us to give consideration to the teachings of our Master.

Jesus tells us that our heavenly Father's opinion about who we are is all that truly matters. If He approves of us, that's all the approval we need. He gives us our identity and an inner beauty that far surpasses anything related to what we might wear, own, drive, or live in.

As for performance, what more does our heavenly Father expect of us than that we do our best? We are responsible to prepare carefully, and then to step out and work hard!

For many years I was afraid of disappointing God by not performing up to His high standards (whatever those were), but now I know we cannot disappoint God.

A person can disobey God—either willfully or unknowingly—but he cannot disappoint God. A person can sin or rebel against God, and reap God's consequences for that sin as a means of chastisement. But a person cannot disappoint God.

Stop to think about it for a moment. A God who can be disappointed is a God who loves conditionally—a God who loves us when we perform well, and then withdraws His love if we perform badly. The truth of God's love is that His love is unconditional. He loves us at all times with an infinite, overwhelming, merciful, gracious, passionate love! God's embrace of love doesn't change based upon our performance. On occasion we may feel inadequate and incapable of successfully completing an assignment, but that doesn't have to be a permanent, continuous feeling for us. God can and will help us.

A person can disobey God—either willfully or unknowingly— but a person cannot disappoint God.

He may whisper to our hearts, "I can help you do better than that. I created you to do better than that. I desire that you do better than that." Even as He whispers these messages to our hearts, He is holding us close and valuing us beyond measure. God never withdraws His presence or His love from His children.

My fear of failure was rooted in lack of understanding God's unconditional love. It was rooted in my lack of knowing that God at all times considered me worthy and valuable. It was rooted in my lack of awareness that I could never disappoint God and God would never reject me or withdraw His presence from me.

Have you come to the place in your life that you truly know God loves you, and that nothing you do or say puts you beyond the realm of God's infinite, unconditional love? If you know with certainty this great love of God, then you also know that while you may disappoint yourself or others, you cannot disappoint God. He will never leave you, forsake you, or turn away from you.

Our part is to trust God and acknowledge Him in all things. His part is to lead and guide us in the paths He wants us to pursue.

4. Striving to Follow the World's Pattern

The world tells us that we will feel secure and be free of all anxiety if we just have enough money in our bank accounts, investment portfolios, or our retirement accounts. That just isn't true. There's no lasting security in money, stocks, bonds, or any other form of financial investment.

The world tells us that we will feel secure if we just get our house mortgages fully paid. Not true. No house is ever fully secure against natural disaster, fire, or vandalism.

The world tells us that we will feel secure if we just follow a certain health regimen. Not true. Even very physically fit and apparently healthy people have accidents, contract infectious diseases, and are subject to life-threatening illnesses.

The world tells us that we will feel secure and be free of anxiety in our careers if we are promoted to positions that are high enough in the company or we achieve a certain degree of fame. That also isn't true. Any movie actor or actress will tell you that you are only as famous as your last successful movie or play. Any business executive will tell you that in today's business world, CEOs, top executives, and upper-management employees are sometimes more likely to lose their jobs than many lower-on-the-ladder employees.

The truth is that the world has no magic solution for 100 percent security in any area of life. Only Jesus can give a person the confidence of security deep within.

A person said to me not long ago, "Well, back to reality . . . I dread going back to the office."

I asked, "Don't you enjoy your work?"

"No," he admitted. "I really don't. I like the product we manufacture and I like the money I earn and I like the people I work with . . . but I don't enjoy the tasks and the pressure and the responsibility I face from day to day."

"Why don't you find a job you would enjoy getting up and doing every morning?"

He looked at me as if the thought had never even once crossed his mind. "I've got too much at stake in my current position," he said with a great weariness in his voice. "At my age, I doubt that I could be hired at a decent salary by any other company."

"Have you ever stopped to think what you might like to do if you didn't work at the job you presently have?"

His eyes brightened. "Sure," he said. But then his shoulders slumped and the light went out of his eyes. "But that's only a daydream. Maybe I'll get to do that in another ten years when I retire."

I felt sorry for this man as I watched him leave. To think of awaking each morning and going through the motions of a job only for the money seems like sheer drudgery. Such a job is a burden, not a blessing. And the greater the burden associated with any responsibility, the greater the tension, frustration, and anxiety. Furthermore, there's plenty of opportunity for regret to settle in.

If this man doesn't begin to pursue the God-given dreams that reside deep in his heart, he's going to find himself saying in the future, "I regret I spent my life doing what I did. I wish I had taken a different path." He will especially feel that way if he develops health problems that keep him from pursuing his dream when he retires in ten years.

If you are stuck in a job or a situation that is overly tedious, boring, exhausting, or that involves constant struggle—make a change! I'm not talking about having a tedious day or a boring week or a tiring couple of weeks as you bring a project to conclusion. Every job has certain moments and periods that are more demanding than others. I'm talking about a job that has very little exhilaration and joy associated with it—a job that seems to drain you without giving back much satisfaction or fulfillment. A job with no internal reward, only an external paycheck, is not a job worth the time and energy of your life.

Ask God what He would have you do, and start getting the information and training for doing that work. Begin to develop the necessary skills for your "dream job." Put out applications for employment in that field.

If you believe you are in the job God has given to you, but you find it a constant drain on your emotions, energy, and creativity, ask God to help you develop a new attitude toward your work. Ask Him to show you His higher purposes for your being where He has placed you. Begin to see your job as a God-given opportunity.

5. LIVING IN THE TOMORROW

One of the foremost causes of anxiety is a desire for the good things of the future to arrive. Today many children live in this distraction—they long to be grown up, or to "finally" be a teenager, or to get out on their own. Other people fear the future. Generally, those who have a negative view of God's trustworthiness and of life in general have a desire to get into tomorrow so they can get the bad stuff of today behind them. They are worried about what will happen in the near future or the distant future, and they miss out on the fullness of today because they are anxious about tomorrow.

A person may say:

"Suppose I don't get into the college of my choice . . ."

"Suppose I don't get the job I want . . ."

"Suppose I get fired . . ."

"Suppose the person I love doesn't love me back . . ."

"Suppose the people who are invited to my party don't show up or don't have a good time . . ."

"Suppose something comes up to keep me from leaving for my vacation on time . . ."

Friend, the God who is in control of today is also the God who is fully in control of tomorrow. He has already prepared for what will happen to you! He has already provided what you will need tomorrow. He has already anticipated the problems you will face tomorrow and set into motion everything required to resolve those problems.

The God who is in control of today is also the God who is fully in control of tomorrow.

You cannot predict tomorrow. You cannot fully prepare for all contingencies. You cannot fully provide for all you'll need in your future. God not only can, He already has! God is never caught off guard. He is never taken by surprise. He never comes up short. So you do not have to live with anxiety about the future. The peace-filled heart is the one that recognizes "My times are in His hands."

God desires that we view our troubles, whether present concerns or those looming in the future, from His perspective. We are not to deny them or seek to escape them, but rather to regard them as trials and tribulations that we must overcome.

God never expects us to put up with constant anxiety. He intends for us to confront those situations that make us anxious, to face up to the anxiety we have allowed to fill our hearts, and to come to grips with the agitation we feel inside. He intends for us to resist the tendency to worry or become fearful and to refuse to lay down our peace no matter what the devil sends our way.

I don't know that a person ever becomes immune to anxiety. But I am confident of this: It would take a lot to make me anxious now. When I look back over my life, I realize that things that once upset me don't bother me as much now. Things that once caused me to feel anxious don't cause anxiety now. I also know that the more a person trusts God to meet his deep inner needs, the more his faith is going to grow, and the quicker he will be able to trust the Lord in all situations.

I encourage you today . . .

- Refuse to allow anxiety to become a "state of being" in your life.

- Believe God when He says you are worthy of His constant care.

- Yield total control of every area of your life to God.

- Refuse to be caught up in what others think of you.

- Refuse to be trapped into operating according to the world's systems.

- Get your priorities in line with God's priorities for you.

- Choose to live in today, not tomorrow.

And you will find yourself living with a growing deep inner peace.

∞

TEN

Living in Peace with Others

The apostle Paul wrote a very forthright and practical directive to his friends in Rome. He told them to, as much as possible, try to live at peace with everybody. Sometimes that might
be a challenge.

It seems almost inevitable that we all will have neighbors or
acquaintances who are not easy to get along with. Some of them
would probably say the same about you. Nevertheless, we are
encouraged to do all that we can to live peacefully with all men
and women.

The implication is that it is not going to be possible in all situations to be at peace with every person. Paul says "if" it is possible, and "as much as depends on you." There are some people
who simply will not live at peace with you, regardless of what
you do or don't do.

God knows our human nature. He knows that we will be at
odds with other people from time to time, even other followers
of Jesus who are our brothers and sisters in the faith. His challenge
to us is this: Don't let the fault for a lack of peace be the result of
something *you* have done.

The importance of this directive can be seen in the story of a man named Brian who lived in Illinois. As a strapping young man in his early twenties, Brian's life had dramatically changed when God spoke to him, and he responded in faith and commitment. For several years Brian was a faithful and forceful Christian until a fateful event occurred. He had a confrontation with someone in his local church, and he was offended. He said, "I will never go back to church because of this affront," and at the same time, he abandoned his walk with God. For the next forty years he lived with the bitterness and anger of that sad moment until, in his sixties, he was pruning a tree in his yard. His house was only one block from the church he had abandoned years previously.

As he was in the branches, he distinctly heard God's voice say to him, "Brian, you have ignored My voice to you over these many years. This is the last time I will call on you to forgive those who hurt you and to repent of your bitterness and anger."

Brian realized that this was his last opportunity to mend fences with his church and with his God. So immediately he went down to the church and publicly repented and asked forgiveness. For the remaining years of his life, Brian was the pillar of the church—always there, always serving, always caring for others. He often reminisced on the fact that he had sadly lost forty-odd years of joy because of his foolish mistake.

GETTING RID OF A SELF-FIRST ATTITUDE

Pride and self-centeredness were at the core of Brian's problem. It devastated his relationship with others and his own inner well-being. Pride is difficult to lay down. It is at the core of the persona. It is not our normal human instinct to be selfless, giving, or generous toward others.

Sharing is one of the first lessons every parent attempts to teach his or her child. From birth, babies want what they want, and if they don't get what they want when they want it, they cry—and sometimes scream or whine. It is the rare child who desires to share a favorite toy or a chocolate-chip cookie with another toddler. Sometimes a young child will grip an item so tightly in his or her refusal to give it up that a real tug-of-war can develop between a parent and child.

That instinct of "self first" stays with us. It isn't automatically removed when we become Christians. God does not remove self or pride from us as if by some spiritual surgery. Self-focused pride is something that we must lay down, give up, or yield to the Lord. Learning to serve others, to lay down our lives for others, is a principle clearly taught in the Scriptures, but it is never taught as though it were an easy lesson to learn. In this area of laying down our own rights for the sake of someone else, there seems to be no easy answer.

When Brian made the decision to allow unresolved bitterness and anger to reside in his heart, he became a prisoner to the events that followed—broken relationships, severed ties with his church and most of all, a long-term spirit of defiance and arrogance toward the God who had offered him His peace and salvation. In other words, Brian became a man who lost his peace—his peace and God's peace.

Brian's story illustrates how easy it is to allow issues of various kinds to damage or destroy our peace.

SURFACE ISSUES CAN CAUSE DESTRUCTIVE CONFLICT

Pride runs deep, but a number of other issues that are more on the surface can also be destructive to peace and cause conflict in our lives. The difference is that pride *automatically* results in conflict. These surface issues do not *need* to produce conflict. They cause conflict only because we allow them to do so. These are issues that can be resolved or curtailed in such a way that they do not become divisive.

Here are four of these troubling issues:

1. PERSONALITY CONFLICTS

Brian's issues were not based on personality conflicts. He felt maligned and falsely accused by someone in his church, but it really doesn't matter if a relationship is broken or marred because of any type of conflict—the result is always bad!

Certainly not all of us are alike, have the same style, enjoy the same things, think, or act alike. We do have differences in our personalities. But a personality conflict should never erupt in a feud or a war. A personality conflict is not a good reason to shut out another person, criticize him, or seek vengeance against him. Admit that you are different as human beings. Be kind and courteous; and go on down the road. Seek out people whose company you enjoy. But don't shut a door of ministry or refuse to help another person just because you don't like his personality.

A person once said to me, "I don't think God expects me to get along with people who have a personality I don't like."

Yes, He does.

Getting along with a person should have nothing to do with personality. There's no place in Scripture where personality negates our obligation to show kindness, mercy, forgiveness, civility, or good manners! Personality should make no more difference than age, race, sex, culture, nationality, or any other defining factor.

How many people do you know who married a person who was just like them in personality? The fact is, a high percentage of people marry people who *aren't* like them. The old saying "Opposites attract" is very often true. That doesn't necessarily mean that "opposites live together well." Those things that attract us to another person—those traits that aren't like who we are and are, therefore, interesting and intriguing to us—are sometimes traits that we find very difficult to live with.

> **The old saying "Opposites attract" is very often true. That doesn't necessarily mean that "opposites live together well."**

On the other hand, differences can be very beneficial and enriching. They can force us out of our comfort zones and cause us to stretch and grow. They can challenge us to be better than we have been, do more than we have done, and pursue higher goals than we had previously set for our lives. Differences can add real spice to a relationship.

2. Differences in Opinion

What holds true for personality conflicts also holds true for those who have differences of opinion.

At times, the most interesting conversations are ones in which two people have a difference of opinion or viewpoint. The people involved may very well have had differences in upbringing or past experiences. Conversations that involve differences can be very enlightening, enjoyable, and energizing.

It is when we allow hatred, anger, resentment, or bitterness to creep into our differences that we are in danger of destroying a relationship. You are responsible for guarding against the developing of hatred, anger, resentment, or bitterness in *your* heart.

The way you feel toward another person is not an automatic consequence of what that person did—it is a matter of what you have allowed *yourself* to feel.

We don't necessarily need to agree with others on every point of every issue in order to have a productive, meaningful, enjoyable, and purposeful relationship with that person. If so, I doubt that any of us would have long-term friendships, or marriages for that matter. The truth is we all are different human beings with differing perspectives, ideals, and ideas about our world, but those differences should not cause brokenness among us. We should be able to live in peace with each other. One valuable trait that will enable people of differing values to have satisfactory friendships with each other is if they have loyalty toward each other. Loyalty allows us to disagree on certain things and yet be committed to our friendship and a long-term association.

Throughout Christendom, sadly, there are many, diverse denominations, churches, and factions. Often, these divisions have occurred because somewhere in the history of the movement some of the key players disagreed on the interpretation of the Scriptures or on some theological issue.

Some of these differences were totally unnecessary. All Christians do not need to believe *exactly* the same thing about all passages in the Bible. There are some subjects that are impossible for us to reach agreement about because there's no way of proving one particular idea or perspective is the correct one.

Let me give you an example of this.

When I was in Bible school, several friends and I would find ourselves arguing periodically over what the Bible says about the end times. Some would say, "The Lord is coming back soon!" and they'd cite Scriptures as evidence that the Lord's return was imminent. Others would say, "He can't come that soon—all these things must be fulfilled first" . . . and they'd cite several scriptural passages to support their viewpoint. Still others would say, "We can't know! Even Jesus said that He didn't know the day or the hour of His return to earth, only God the Father!"

These discussions late at night in the dorms or in a café over a cheeseburger and milk shake were lively, sometimes fairly heated, vigorous, and even fun. But in the end . . . none of us could *guarantee* that we were right. We believed what we believed. None of us could prove our points because the proof will come only *after* the people of God are taken to heaven to be with Him forever.

Were my buddies and I still friends after an entire evening of arguing over the timetable of the end times? Most definitely. Our argument had nothing to do with the ongoing nature of our deep friendship.

Should such theological disagreements divide the body of Christ? Absolutely not. There's so much that needs to be done to teach others about His plan for their lives. We need to lay down any doctrinal differences that keep us from working together toward that end. What brings us together is the message that Jesus offers salvation to all who believe in Him.

By the way, friend, from time to time, you may discover that a person you had disagreed with is *right*. Even though it is often hard for us to admit, on occasion we are dead wrong! Yes, all of us are wrong from time to time. In a particular situation, you may have thought you had all the facts or wisdom you needed to reach a right decision or make a right choice, only to discover that you did not have the whole story. If that's the case, don't hang on to error out of pride. Admit you were wrong. Choose to learn and adapt and grow!

3. DIFFERENCES IN STYLE AND METHODOLOGY

From time to time you are going to encounter people you like, and who believe as you do, but who disagree with you over a particular approach, decision-making protocol, methodology, or style choice.

A number of years ago, I discovered that a man who worked with me at In Touch Ministries had a very different organizational style than I had when it came to the way he ordered his office. Or perhaps I should say, failed to order his office. His office had no organizational order to it that I could detect!

When I'm studying for a sermon or am in the midst of researching a project, I may have any number of reference books and papers open and scattered about me. But at the end of the day, those books and papers find a home. I don't function well with a lot of clutter surrounding me. This man seemed to thrive on clutter. His desk was piled high with papers and books and file folders jumbled together in piles here and there all over his office.

And yet, this man produced an amazing amount of work. He seemed to know precisely what was in each pile. If I asked him for a particular piece of information, he had an uncanny way of reaching into a stack of papers and files about two-thirds of the way down and pulling out the exact item I wanted. I came to the conclusion that we had a big difference in style, but that difference didn't keep us from working well together.

I also knew that I had absolutely no hope of ever convincing this man that he needed to have a less cluttered office. Neither did he have any hope of convincing me that my style of work was less desirable than his. We agreed to disagree on this matter. And thankfully, whenever we held an open house, he kindly shut his door without ever being asked!

From time to time people are going to disagree on methodology. In those cases, the person responsible for the success of the project should be the person responsible for choosing the method by which you'll conduct the project. If you can't agree with the method a leader chooses to use, you may help the leader by suggesting a new approach. But if the person who is in authority over you concludes that he is going to do it the way he feels is the best, then you are better off agreeing to work the plan his way, or else you may need to find a new job. Differences in methodology are no cause for frustration, hatred, anger, or division. Please don't let a matter of style rob you of your peace.

4. COMMUNICATION ERRORS

On occasion, we experience distress because of a failure to communicate well. Sometimes people don't state their positions or directions clearly, or hear accurately what is being said. So often we hear what we want to hear. At other times, we only hear part of what has been said—and it is usually the part that we like or want to believe.

I can't tell you the times I've preached only to have people come to me afterward and tell me that they really liked one particular thing that I said. Many times what they *heard* me say was not what I said at all! They had heard something that made them feel good, that bolstered what they already believed, or that gave them justification for doing what they already wanted to do.

What about anger in conversation? Let me quickly point out that angry eruptions are *not* a godly communication style. If a person has a hot temper, he needs to recognize that he doesn't have peace deep inside. "But that's just the way God made me," some people say. No, it's not the way God made you. It may be the way your parents influenced you or it may result from some learned behavior patterns as you were growing up, but it certainly is not what God intends. He is the God of peace. You are to be a person of peace. Anger in all forms is a means of destroying peace. The brother of our Lord, James, said, "for the wrath of man does not produce the righteousness of God" (James 1:20).

Erupting from time to time in a temper tantrum may be a habit you have had for many years, even from childhood. But having a volatile temper is not the way God designed you.

A person with a volatile, hot temper is like a volcano. That molten lava of anger is always burning deep within, and occasionally that flow of anger vents and spews all over others. A hot-tempered person is not a joy to be around.

We make a grave mistake if we think that having a temper is a sign of strength—of boldness, of strong determination, of a

get-with-it and make-it-happen character trait. Those who believe this tend to think of peaceful people as being laid-back, not
very ambitious, perhaps lazy, and people who are just willing to
"go with the flow." These are false perceptions.

A person can be bold, determined, and have a driving energy
to reach God-given goals and never once shout at other people,
throw a tantrum, cry, hit anything, or even clench a fist. A person
can feel relaxed, have a quiet confidence, and be at peace, and not
be the least bit lazy. A peaceful person is not necessarily a person
who compromises readily—and certainly a *godly*, peaceful person
is never a person who compromises with evil in any form it may
take.

Peace is not passive. Peace is active—it is positive, motivating,
and exhilarating.

Are you misinterpreting? Sometimes it is easy to become upset
and lose our peace when we feel we have been misunderstood.
Do you ever feel rejection when somebody voices something
that you interpret as criticism? It is not easy, but if you are committed to living at peace with others, be willing to recognize that
it is not difficult to misread the intent of other people's words
and actions.

**Peace is not passive. Peace is active—it is positive, motivat-
ing, and exhilarating.**

In other words, the road to peace is often paved with the spirit
of giving others the benefit of your doubt! This can lead to your
saying "thank you" to someone for his correction rather than

assuming the individual did not have your best interest in mind when he corrected you. The writer of Proverbs said, "As iron sharpens iron so a man sharpens the countenance of his friend" (27:17).

For some of us, to be misunderstood is a painful issue. I feel especially hurt when I know that I have been misunderstood. When someone has not understood the intent of my heart or my motive, and then speaks negatively to me or about me—that is painful! In spite of my best efforts and willingness to communicate, that sometimes happens. Do I try to restate what I believe or advise so that I am better understood? Yes. Do I always succeed in that? No. The result is a wounding of my heart, even if the other person didn't intend to wound me.

Make sure that you are not misinterpreting what others are saying. Ask for clarification.

If you believe you are being misunderstood, seek to explain, clarify, or restate your meaning or your motives. Don't give in to anger or give up in disgust. Keep trying to communicate!

Remember, we are not always surrounded by friends, so there will be times when we can expect to be bombarded by occasional "fiery darts"—insults, critical comments, ridicule, or words of rejection. Sometimes these words are hurled directly at you in a spirit of revenge, hate, or anger. Sometimes you hear about things indirectly. At times, these stinging comments are made out of jealousy or as an attempt to undermine your success. The bombardment may be sporadic and occasional . . . in cases of emotional abuse, the bombardment may be nearly constant. These attacks can be cruel and devastating. Do not fall into the trap of thinking that the old childhood rhyme that says, "Sticks and stones may break my bones but words will never hurt me," is true—it isn't.

Fiery-dart comments hurt. They wound us. There's no escaping them, and no escaping the wounding they cause unless we totally shut ourselves off from other people, which isn't what God desires for us. No, these moments are opportunities for us to experience the power and presence of God in our lives, which can enable us to have peace in the midst of persecution.

The good news is that Jesus said, "Blessed are you when they revile and persecute you, and say all kinds of evil against you falsely for My sake. Rejoice and be exceedingly glad, for great is your reward in heaven . . ." (Matt. 5:11–12).

I want you to see two things in what Jesus said. First, He said that we are blessed when people say evil things against us *falsely*. If there's truth in the criticism that is flung your way, don't turn your back on that truth. Take it to heart and ask God how He would have you change your attitude or behavior. There's no blessing in doing something that is an error, sin, or act of unrighteousness, then ignoring or denying what you have done. There's blessing only in what you do that is good and right before God.

Second, Jesus said we are blessed if people speak evil against us falsely *for His sake*. Blessing comes to us when we are living out what God has called us to do, and others criticize us for heeding *His* words and obeying *His* plan and purpose for our lives.

The question is not whether we are going to be wounded in life by what others say, but whether we are going to hang on to the hurt and keep picking at the wound so that it never heals. Do we continue to hold resentment or bitterness in our hearts toward the person who has spoken evil against us? Do we shun that person or shut our ears to anything further he or she may say to us? Do we distance ourselves from the person?

> **Blessing comes to us when we are living out what God has called us to do, and others criticize us for heeding *His* words and obeying *His* plan and purpose for our lives.**

God's Word calls us to respond to hurtful comments by speaking well of and doing good to the person who insults or criticizes us. The Bible calls us to pray for the person who hurts us. Doing this draws our focus away from our hurt feelings and on to something positive and beneficial. We also are wise to ask the Lord to heal our hearts—showing us any lesson we might learn from the wounding we have experienced. We must ask the Lord to help us forgive the other person. And then, knowing that we have done all the Lord has asked of us . . . and fully expecting Him to heal us, restore us, and strengthen us . . . we must move forward with confidence and faith and His peace.

Remember Brian? He responded wrongly to an ugly event in his life, and he rejected God's directive—to forgive and be healed by God's grace. Instead, he chose to do the "normal" thing—he decided that he would take things into his own hands and nurture a spirit of anger and bitterness in his soul. As a result, he lived without God's presence and peace all those years except for the moments when God's Spirit would visit him and urge him to forgive and repent of his anger. Finally, he knew he had one final opportunity, and thank God, he took it.

From that day forward, everyone who knew him realized that he was a new man—changed in countenance and spirit. He became a man of peace—with himself, with others, and with God. In the next chapter we will learn how we can restore broken relationships with others—just as Brian did.

ELEVEN

RESTORING PEACE
IN RELATIONSHIPS

A challenge each of us regularly faces is: How can we live in peace with other people and restore peace when conflict erupts? The fact is, God desires that we live in peace with others. He also knows that we will not always be at peace with others. Conflicts occur. At times, conflicts are not easily resolved. In fact, there are occasions when conflicts *cannot* be resolved. As noted in the previous chapter, however, God does want us to do all we can to be at peace with everyone.

We who are followers of Jesus know full well that when God is not in full control of our lives, we can act just as despicably as an unbeliever. Our salvation does not automatically keep us from being mean, jealous, hateful, or angry. It is only as we ask the Holy Spirit to work in us and through us, only as we yield our nature to His nature, only as we seek to be His representative on this earth in every relationship we have that we are going to move beyond pride into the behaviors that establish peace.

So often people aren't willing to take responsibility for their actions. When a dispute arises, many people settle into the excuse

"I can't help it. That's just the way I am." It never dawns on them that they can *change* the way they are, or that God desires for them to do just that!

I am reminded of the son of one of my friends. He was in junior high school, and one morning he didn't want to go to school. He said to his dad, "This is going to be a bad day. I just know bad things will happen. I don't feel good, and things are going to get worse. Dad, I can just feel it in my bones."

His father said, "Son, your problem is that you have your radio tuned to the wrong station. You have to change the dial to a more positive station. Why don't you do that?" His son, without any qualms, said, "My hand doesn't want to do it." At that point he gestured to his father, showing how his quaking hand was unable to turn the dial.

That little story tells it all—choosing the right course of action, especially one that may cause us to lose face or feel shame for our part in a dispute, is probably the last thing we want to do, but it is the foundation stone of being at peace with others. It is the *heart* of the matter. I focus on the word *heart* because it is key to being at peace.

HAVING THE RIGHT HEART FOR PEACE

God is the ultimate answer to any difficulties you may have in the area of dispute or conflict with others. What is the first thing you should do if you find that you are unable to resolve a difference or reconcile a disagreement in peace? Go to God with the problem. Don't go running to your friends. They may or may not give you good advice. Go to God's Word. If you do this, remember in the most well-known prayer Jesus taught to His followers that He told them to ask their heavenly Father to forgive them as they forgave others! As you are looking to God for help, you may also feel the need to ask a godly counselor for some wise advice.

As you seek God's directives, give yourself a heart check. See if you have . . .

A PURE HEART

When you are seeking for peace, the proper attitude to have is a pure heart. Jesus taught, "Have salt in yourselves, and have peace with one another" (Mark 9:50). This is a direct reference to purity. At that time, salt was the purest substance known to man. It came from the purest sources—the sea and the sun. A pure heart results in your wanting only what God wants, which is all things that are of eternal benefit. In other words, you want others around you to follow Jesus, grow spiritually, be transformed, and be blessed in all ways. Those with a pure heart desire what God desires more than what they personally want.

A LOVING HEART

Loving is always expressed by giving. Not all gifts are given with love, but all genuine love results in a spontaneous flow of giving—giving in words, in deeds, in objects, in other signs of affection. Love allows you to look beyond a person's actions and find a godly way to *give* to that person.

At times, the greatest act of love may be a gift of forgiveness, or it may be godly advice or admonition. It may be the gift of an encouraging word or genuine compliment. It may be a gift that meets a specific need for security, comfort, health, or sustenance in another person's life. A loving heart always looks toward the highest and greatest expression of God's love in a relationship. It is love that is unconditional and overflowing.

> **Loving is always expressed by giving. Not all gifts are given with love, but all genuine love results in a spontaneous flow of giving—giving in words, in deeds, in objects, in other signs of affection.**

A PATIENT HEART

Colossians 3:12–13 tells us to "put on tender mercies, kindness, humility, meekness, longsuffering; bearing with one another, and forgiving one another." To be long-suffering means to be patient. In purity, and with a loving heart, we are to be patient with the other person in a relationship, giving God time to work in his or her life. We must be willing to endure some tough times, some criticism, and even some times when we may not be able to discern clearly what God is doing. We need to be willing to wait until God says, "Act now."

A FORGIVING HEART

Jesus said, "Forgive, and you will be forgiven" (Luke 6:37). The apostle Paul wrote, "If anyone has a complaint against another; even as Christ forgave you, so you also must do" (Col. 3:13). Forgiveness means that we are willing to let go of the pain we feel, and give it to God. We are willing to place every hurt and injustice into the hands of God and trust Him to heal our hearts and deal with those who have wounded us.

We must *always* forgive. There is never any situation in which unforgiveness can be justified before God. Forgiveness does not mean that we deny our injuries, dismiss our pain, or lay aside all claims to justice. It *does* mean that we must release that person from our own judgment and let go of any bitterness or feelings of revenge.

Should the other person decide to walk away from your relationship, you are not responsible for his action.

Should the other person decide to leave your employment, you are not responsible for her decision.

Should the other person decide to continue to treat you with contempt, criticism, condemnation, or cruel behavior, you are not responsible for his behavior.

Do all that you know to do to live in peace with others—with a pure, loving, patient, and forgiving heart—and you will have done what God requires of you. This foundation, then, prepares you for any situation in which broken relationships are threatening to capsize your boat.

Except for the man who has trouble forgiving himself for some past transgression, inevitably, in any conflict there are at least two people involved—often many more. With this in mind it is important to remind ourselves that without exception, reconciliation is always a matter of choice; and, conversely, living in peace with others to the best of your ability is always a choice. Did you notice what I said? "To the best of your ability"—that means if you choose to put out your best effort, you can be at peace.

RECONCILIATION IS A CHOICE WE MAKE

Living in peace with another person is a choice you make.

In your friendships . . .

In your relationship with your parents or children . . .

In your marriage . . .

In your neighborhood . . .

In your workplace . . .

In your church . . .

Make peace a *priority* choice. Value peace. Choose to seek it until you find it.

Don't expect any relationship to be peaceful at all times, however. Expect conflict to arise, but then also expect that in the vast majority of cases, you will be able to find a way to work through the conflict.

So many times a couple will marry thinking that everything in their relationship is going to be fantastic. They believe this because they interact well with one another, and their financial and social statuses seem to mesh nicely together. The specter of broken promises and broken marriages all across America attests that this isn't necessarily so. Experience tells us that unless those two people come to the point where they learn how to love each other and live in genuine peace, all the money, status, and possessions in this world can't produce a good marriage.

When people are in positions of authority in their company or organization and they believe that "leadership" requires them to run roughshod over people and to bully others into doing their bidding, they are in for a fall. Ungodly behavior cannot produce genuine blessing. Being a firm, responsible, diligent, and faithful leader . . . yes! But being unkind, unappreciative, unwilling to listen, fostering feuds and conflicts in an attempt to motivate people toward better performance . . . no! Ungodly behavior will always produce strife, and strife always results in a lowering of quality, productivity, and morale. A godly leader will seek to create an environment in which people can work in peace toward a common goal.

Don't fall into the trap of thinking that conflict is required for progress in either a relationship or an organization.

Seek peace.

DEALING WITH MAJOR CONFLICTS

How do we deal with a major conflict when it arises?

DETERMINE THE VALUE OF THE RELATIONSHIP

First, if you are going to live in peace with another person, you have to decide, "Is this relationship valuable enough to me to preserve it? Am I willing to compromise on some things to make the relationship work? Is this relationship valuable enough for me to do what is necessary to *learn* to live in peace with this person or group of people?"

At times, your answer may be no. You may reach the conclusion that the pain involved in sustaining that friendship isn't worth your time and energy. If that's the case, then, as best you can, walk away in peace.

I recently heard about a woman named Margo who became friends with a woman named Carol. After several months of having dinner or going to a movie with Carol every week or so,

Margo began to feel uncomfortable. Carol began calling her more and more, depending upon her for more and more emotional support, and insisting on spending more and more time with her. Others began to tell Margo that they thought Carol was obsessed with her. Friends reported that Carol had snapshots of Margo all over her apartment and that she had told a mutual friend that she couldn't imagine living without Margo in her life.

Margo knew she needed to back away from the friendship. She tried to talk to Carol about what it meant to be friends. She suggested Carol talk to a Christian counselor about how to establish an appropriate friendship. Carol became very defensive and refused that suggestion. Margo then said she would need to end their relationship, at which point Carol became almost violent in her insistence that the friendship be maintained. In the end, Margo had to hire a bodyguard because of Carol's threats and continued stalking.

Now that is an extreme situation, but it points to the reality that not all relationships are healthy, and not all friendships that seem to start out being healthy can be sustained in a healthy manner. Some people simply do not know *how* to be friends, supportive colleagues, loyal employees, helpful employers, or kind neighbors.

The extent to which you consider a relationship to be valuable or important—and healthy and mutually satisfying—is very likely the degree to which you are going to be willing to make compromises necessary to maintain the relationship. Determine how much you *value* a relationship, and then choose the extent to which you will go to preserve that relationship.

I firmly believe that two people who are saved by the grace of God and indwelled by the same Holy Spirit can find genuine peace in their relationship if they both genuinely value the maintenance of the relationship.

START TALKING AND KEEP TALKING

When two people are talking, and they are willing to keep on talking to each other and *listening* to each other, they are much more likely to come to a resolution. Real understanding is rarely achieved in cold silence!

> **The words *but, if,* and *when* insert conditions into a relationship, and genuine love is unconditional.**

Don't tell me that you love another person, but you are unwilling to talk to that person. Don't tell me that you love another person, but you just can't open up and be transparent about your feelings, ideas, or your past experiences. Don't tell me that you love another person, but you are unwilling to work on getting to the core issue of a problem that exists between you. Any time you say, "I love her, *but* . . ." or "I love him *when* . . ." you have just told me that you don't really love that person or value that relationship. The words *but, if,* and *when* insert conditions into a relationship, and genuine love is unconditional. Genuine love never limits conversation, transparency, or personal self-examination. Genuine love is marked by generous giving and a willingness to change, grow, mature, and *share* the fullness of life with another person.

When one person clams up, pulls down the shade on emotional involvement, and stubbornly refuses to discuss an issue any further, a relationship is damaged. Any time a wall of defense begins to be built with the prevailing attitude "I don't want to hear anything you have to say on this matter," there's very little hope of achieving peace. There is a young married couple, friends of a friend, who are finding marriage a tough go. The disheartening thing about them is that both the man and the woman do not seem ready to invest themselves in saving the relationship. Both of them appear to be preoccupied with their own self-interests, and the result is disenchantment and disillusionment for both of them.

On the other hand, if two people are willing to keep talking, keep discussing, keep open to each other, and keep listening, those two people have a real chance of reaching a mutually satisfying agreement and a peaceful resolution of their differences. That doesn't mean one person does all the talking and the other does the listening. A mutuality of talking and listening is required.

Words such as *command, demand, order,* or *insist* have no part in a discussion. Neither do threats, whether veiled or clearly stated. An attitude of "It's my way or the highway" doesn't produce peace.

Two people with differences need to learn to seek *understanding*—which is more than mere information. They need to get to the heart of a disagreement, including motives, desires, and needs that may not have been spoken. They need to be honest about their own emotions and be clear in stating what they would like the nature of the relationship to be or become.

> **Two people with differences need to learn to seek *under-standing*—which is more than mere information.**

BE TRANSPARENT

You can't have a hidden agenda or a manipulative scheme at work in the back of your mind and hope for a peaceful relationship. Sooner or later, your agenda and manipulation are going to be felt, even if not openly recognized, and the other person's reaction is likely to be one of defensive withdrawal or open hostility.

I know of an executive working in Atlanta for a foreign firm who was involved in a dispute over the leasing agreement his firm had with the owner of the building. Neither party agreed to the other's position, and there was a significant amount of money in dispute.

The executive, a growing follower of Jesus, did something I highly admired. He sat across the table from the owner and his lawyer and wrote out a check made payable to the owner . . . only he did not write in the amount of money. He passed the check to the owner and said, "I believe you will follow a course of integrity. I am relying on you to fill in the amount you believe is fair to both of us." With that, the owner and his lawyer withdrew from the discussions. Later they came back, and they had written in the amount of money that was acceptable to the executive.

This man's confidence in God and his determination to live in peace with the owner of the building won the day. He offered transparency and received peace by choosing to risk the loss of a significant sum of money.

Are you willing to admit your mistakes? Are you willing to confess your weaknesses and faults? Are you willing to own up to the fact that you may have misunderstood the other person? Are you willing to admit that you may have overreacted or operated out of pent-up anger?

Are you also willing to look at your own behavioral habits and deeply entrenched attitudes, some of which were engrained since childhood. Not everything we acquire as children is helpful to us as adults. None of us had perfect parents, and therefore, none of us had perfect childhoods.

Have you sorted out fully what was helpful, godly, healthful, and wise from your childhood, and what wasn't? Have you taken responsibility for your own attitudes, opinions, feelings, and behaviors as an adult? Are you willing to admit that some of the ways you relate to another person may be linked to some leftover "baggage" you are carrying from a previous friendship, romantic relationship, or even your early years? Inner and outer transparency can carry the day in helping us relate carefully and lovingly to others. The best way to get a handle on the communication problems created by our weaknesses and failures is to attempt to get to the root of the problem.

GET TO THE CORE PROBLEM

As you communicate openly with another person, with a willingness to be transparent, do your best to get to the problem that may be underlying your disagreement or difference. Ask, "What's the *real* problem?"

Is the core problem related to feelings of low self-worth or an inability to value others? Is the core problem related to pride? Is it related to an inability to overcome rejection or loneliness in a godly manner?

I recently talked to a friend who is a professional psychologist and also a wise, godly woman. She told me a little about her work with a woman who came to her for marriage counseling. She had met fairly regularly with this woman for several months, and she said that it was only recently that this woman was willing to admit to her, "My husband and I haven't shared the same bed in nearly ten years."

"Why not?" this counselor asked.

The woman said, "Well, my husband started coming home from work and immediately exploding in anger. He used terrible language and was extremely hateful about his employer and colleagues. I just couldn't take his angry, emotional outbursts. I'd find myself feeling tied up in knots within a half hour after he got home."

"Was any of his outburst aimed at you?" the counselor asked.

"No. It was all aimed at other people, but it created an atmosphere that I hated. He'd vent all his anger and then act as if nothing was wrong. I felt tense and upset, sometimes to the point I couldn't eat dinner because my stomach was churning so much. It was as if he poured all his anger and frustration into me. Then he'd come to bed three or four hours later and want to be affectionate. I just couldn't change emotional gears that fast. I was still too upset to respond to him."

The counselor then asked, "Did you ever ask him *why* he felt so much anger at work? Did you ever ask him *why* he felt he had the right to vent all that anger in your presence?"

The counselor said to me, "When I asked those questions, this woman just stared at me. She finally admitted that it had never dawned on her to ask those two questions. She had absolutely no clue why this man had such built-up anger in him, or why he thought it was acceptable to explode in anger on a nightly basis in their kitchen. For ten long years the core issue between them had never been addressed. They are so far apart now that it will be a miracle of God for them ever to reconnect."

I asked this counselor what she thought might be the root cause of this man's anger. She told me that based upon her years of counseling experience in similar situations, she suspected that this man's father may have been a man who openly vented hostility and anger, and that this man not only had acquired a bad habit of allowing anger to overtake him, but also had developed bad communication skills. When he felt overlooked, rejected, or confronted at work, he automatically stuffed those feelings and allowed them to be buried inside as anger. Once home, he felt it was "safe" and his "right" to explode at his family.

Now, all those factors she cited are certainly core issues that need to be addressed if that man is going to be healthy emotionally, if his wife is going to be healed of the wounds he has inflicted on her heart, and if their marriage is going to be restored. But he isn't the only person in that relationship.

I asked this counselor, "And what about the woman?"

She replied, "Oh, she has some core issues as well. She's going to have to address why it is that she never asked those questions of him, and why she never once over a period of seven or eight years said to him, 'I've had enough of your ranting and raving. Stop it!' She's going to have to face up to why *she* allowed herself to internalize his anger and become something of an emotional doormat. She's also going to have to face up to the fact that she has used affection and sex as a means of fighting back and manipulating the marriage. I'm not sure she wants to face those things in herself."

"But she came to you for counseling," I said.

"Yes," said this counselor, "but that doesn't mean she came for genuine help. I suspect she may have come so I might validate her secret plan to divorce this man, or perhaps so I might give her some form of justification for her attitudes and behavior. I'll know if she really wants help if she starts making changes in the way *she* communicates and acts."

The counselor said these two people, both with core issues, needed to work on those issues if their marriage was to be saved. I agreed with her. From my experience as a pastor, I can say almost categorically that if one person insists that the root cause of any disagreement resides totally in the other person or insists that the other person do all the changing, or demands that the other person take all responsibility for the failure of a relationship, there's little hope for a peaceful resolution. If a person refuses to address root causes, there's little hope for peace.

On the other hand, if two people are willing to work together to get to the core issues that reside in *both* of them, and which have produced the way in which they communicate and relate to each other, there's great hope for a relationship to be reconciled and sustained in peace.

THE ROLE OF A GODLY COUNSELOR

The Bible tells us that there's great wisdom to be gained from godly counselors (Prov. 11:14). If you and another person with whom you are in conflict both value your relationship enough to make changes, and truly desire to live in peace with each other—but you don't know how to communicate, open up in honest transparency, or get to the core issue of disagreement—go and seek help from a godly counselor. Let me place special emphasis on these two words, *wise* and *godly*.

A wise counselor is one who bases his or her counsel on the Word of God. There's no higher source of wisdom than the Bible.

A godly counselor is a person who truly wants God's best in your life and in your relationship. He wants what Jesus wants for your life. He will point you not only to God's Word, but also to the importance of building any relationship on a mutual love for Christ Jesus. When Jesus is the third person in a relationship—both parties looking to Him as their Savior and seeking to obey Him as their Lord—there's real hope for reconciliation and the establishment of peace.

On the other hand, a counselor who deals only in worldly wisdom is not going to give you the firm foundation you need for a truly peaceful resolution. Bad counsel can destroy a relationship. Go to a person who will point you repeatedly to the Word of God and who will encourage you to pray together and to seek God's will together.

Show me two people who pray together, read and share openly about God's Word together, and who are willing to communicate freely in an open, honest, and transparent way . . . show me two people who each have a deep love for the Lord Jesus . . . show me two people who truly value their relationship and desire God's best for their mutual life . . . and I'll show you two people who have a very strong foundation for reaching agreement and living in a state of abiding peace.

Be willing to work on the relationship.

Be willing to admit your own limitations, failures, and mistakes.

Be willing to talk, and be willing to listen.

Be willing to change your thought patterns, your habitual emotional responses, and your behavior.

RESPONDING TO THOSE WHO HURT US

The apostle Paul gave a very clear admonition of the Lord about how we are to respond to those who hurt us, reject us, or in any way act out of evil intents or motives against us. He said simply, "Repay no one evil for evil" (Rom. 12:17).

Never are we to take vengeance into our own hands. Even in the most difficult of circumstances, we must never seek vengeance. We must leave any retaliation up to the Lord. He knows what is just, and He knows how best and when to heap consequences upon those who do evil to you.

Just this week, I read a story about a remarkable young woman. She was in the Georgia woods on a walking trail when she was shot mistakenly by a hunter. The young man, finding the woman in shock and clearly dying, did everything right from that point on. He gave her artificial respiration, stopped the bleeding, and rushed her to a hospital. He has been charged with felonious assault. She, on the other hand, still very ill in the hospital, has stated publicly that she bears this man no malice. On the contrary, she is asking that he not be prosecuted, and she has expressed her grateful thanks for his helping to save her life. She chose to entrust her well-being into the hands of God. She refused to call for vengeance, and she forgave the man who almost caused her death.

What guidance does God give as to how we should treat our enemies? We are called to trust God with our feelings of anger and vengeance. Paul is very specific:

> If your enemy is hungry, feed him;
> If he is thirsty, give him a drink." (Rom. 12:20)

God promises to reward those who treat their enemies well.

What brings God's reward to *you* is your doing *good* to those who do evil to you. There's no promise of good associated with retaliation, vengeance, or "paying back" a person who has hurt you.

In Bible times, to give food and water to a hungry, thirsty enemy was a sign of tremendous hospitality. People knew that if you turned a hungry, thirsty enemy away from your tent out into the wilderness, that enemy would only seek to do you more harm. Showing basic kindness to the enemy, on the other hand, was a means of defusing his anger and possibly putting a stop to his evil actions.

There's no promise of good associated with retaliation, vengeance, or "paying back" a person who has hurt you.

Food to the hungry and water to the thirsty were examples of meeting very basic needs. There's nothing in the Bible that states we are to go out of our way to make extravagant gestures of generosity to those who do evil to us. We aren't to work for the favor of our enemies, give bribes to them or show favoritism to them. What we are required by God to do is to meet their basic human needs if and when those needs present themselves. We are to be courteous to them, speak kindly to them, and refuse to criticize them.

Jesus said this about our treatment of our enemies: "Love your enemies, bless those who curse you, do good to those who hate you, and pray for those who spitefully use you and persecute you" (Matt. 5:44).

What was true about enemies and persecution in Bible times holds true today! The only possibility of turning an enemy into a friend is by showing kindness to that person. Enemies don't become friends by force or by acts of vengeance. Rather, our enemies become friends when we express the love of God to them, do good to them, speak well of them, and pray for them.

If you show kindness to an enemy, God will reward you. Even if your enemy continues to persecute you and do evil to you, God will find a way to bless you.

Make certain your kindness is genuine and not manipulative. Don't play games with another person. Don't use kindness to get what you want.

When we show kindness to an enemy, that person who has done evil to us is often taken by surprise. He isn't expecting our kindness. He's *expecting* us to act as he acted—to display anger and retaliation and revenge. When we don't act that way, an enemy is much more likely to feel a degree of remorse, anguish, or shame about his actions. This response, in turn, opens up that person to the convicting power of the Holy Spirit. In the end, our act of kindness gives entrance to the Holy Spirit's work in the person's life.

In sharp contrast, when we retaliate against an enemy, we put ourselves on the same plane and in the same camp as the enemy. We are no less guilty of spreading evil. We are no less subject to the consequences of doing evil.

NOT ALL RELATIONSHIPS CAN BE RECONCILED

Not all relationships *can* be reconciled.

"But, Dr. Stanley," you may be saying, "that sounds as if you believe miracles aren't possible in every situation."

I firmly believe in miracles. But I also know that some people don't *want* relationships to be reconciled, and as long as they hold to that position, a relationship cannot be reconciled.

It's simply not possible to reach peaceful resolution of differences if one person in the relationship says flatly, "This is it. I'm out of this relationship. Forget any idea of reconciliation. It's over." One person cannot make a relationship work. One person cannot force another person to choose reconciliation or peace. One person cannot insist that another person stay in a relationship he or she doesn't choose to be in.

A popular Christian psychologist said on one occasion, "In any severed relationship, one of the parties can take the circle 359 degrees, but if the other party refuses for whatever reason to join the circle by going one degree, then the broken relationship cannot be healed."

But why wouldn't a person *want* reconciliation? There are a number of reasons. Some people seem to prefer to live with a high degree of tension, strife, or upheaval. In many cases, these people grew up in a tumultuous environment, and it is the only norm they know. They think they know how to deal with an environment filled with cursing and profanity, occasional violent outbursts, greed, jealousy, or even stonewalling silence, and they become very uncomfortable if there's too much peace or joy.

There are also some people who take pleasure in making other people miserable. They see their ability to inflict pain on another person as a form of power or control. These people feel good only when others around them are feeling bad. They resent anybody who has genuine joy. Ultimately, these people are angry at themselves, but they rarely will admit that self-anger. Then again, conflict to some is the only life they have known. The possibility of peaceful coexistence is an unknown possibility!

BEING AT ODDS IN A MARRIAGE

A man came to me recently and said, "Dr. Stanley, I think my wife is going to leave me. She's been threatening a divorce for several months. I keep asking her what it is that she wants changed in our marriage, but she won't answer me. I think the only thing she wants changed is that she doesn't want to be married to *me*. What can I do to keep my marriage together?"

I said, "You may not be able to keep your marriage together if she doesn't want to stay married to you, or if she can't identify what it is that she thinks is wrong in your marriage."

He replied, "The only thing she says to me is, 'You just don't make me happy anymore.' That makes me think there's something I used to do to make her happy that I don't do now. I can't for the life of me think of what that may be, and when I've asked her, she doesn't have an answer."

"I don't believe you *can* make her happy," I told him.

He became a little defensive. "I think I could," he said. "If I only knew what to do, I'd do it."

"No," I responded, "you can't make her happy. Nobody—not you or anybody else—can make another person happy. Genuine, lasting, satisfying happiness is something that can only be found in a person's relationship with Jesus. You may be able to give your wife a few things or do a few things for her that will bring a temporary smile to her face, but you can't *make* her feel happiness."

"But what about the verses in the Bible that say we have a responsibility for other people—I am to be my brother's keeper, for example. Doesn't that mean I have a responsibility to make my wife happy?"

"Your biblical responsibility as a husband is to love your wife and to give to your wife—to care for her and provide for her just as you do your own self. It means to share with her and build her up and encourage her. How she *receives* what you do is up to her. She can receive all that you do for her and say to her, and appreciate it, value it, and feel joy about it, or she can receive it with a feeling that what you do is not enough and never will be enough. You can't govern her feelings as she receives what you do."

"So I shouldn't keep asking my wife what I can do for her?"

"Of course you can ask her that," I said. "I'm not saying that you shouldn't keep giving to her or loving her. I'm saying that you aren't responsible for how she receives what you give. Happiness is a decision she's going to have to make. Peace in your relationship is a decision she's going to have to make. Thankfulness in her heart for a loving husband and a good family and a beautiful home is something she is going to have to *choose* to feel and express."

He sat for a few moments, reflecting on what I said, and then he sighed and said, "Trying to make her happy has really felt like a burden."

"It is a burden. It's not one we can bear for very long before we collapse under the weight of it. Let me ask you, when was the last time you asked your wife what you could do to help her or encourage her?"

"Last night," he said. "She just glared at me, shrugged her shoulders, and walked off to another room and slammed the door behind her."

"When was the last time she asked *you* what she could do to help you or encourage you?"

He stared blankly back at me. "I don't know that she's ever asked me that question."

"How long have you been married?"

"Fifteen years."

"And she's never asked you what she might do to help you or encourage you?"

"No."

"Did she ever ask that question when you were just dating or courting?"

"No."

"That should have been a clue," I said. "Love is translated into *giving*. When you really love a person, you can't give enough to that person. You want to give. You want to give what the other person takes delight in receiving. The apostle Paul wrote, that love 'does not seek its own.' In other words, it doesn't demand to receive. It seeks to give." (See 1 Cor. 13:5.)

I then told this man about a young couple that I knew many years ago. The bride-to-be told me how excited she was about getting married, and she referred to her fiancé as "the man of my dreams." She went on at some length to tell me about where he worked, what kind of money he was earning, where they were planning to live, and even the type of car he had said he was going to buy for her.

Little warning bells went off inside my head. I asked, "And what is it that you are planning to give and do for him? It sounds as if he's going to be a wonderful husband. What are you going to provide for him?"

She looked at me with a huge question mark on her face. Finally she said, "You mean, like cook dinner?"

I had to laugh. "Well, that's a start," I said. "Love is all about *giving*. Rather than ask yourself, 'What can I get my future husband to give to me and do for me,' you need to be asking yourself, 'What am I eager to give to my future husband and do for him?' A good marriage happens when both the wife and the husband are generous givers to each other. Real love means you can't ever seem to give enough. It's not about getting; it's about unselfishly giving."

She walked away from that brief conversation with her shoulders slumped. I felt as if I had just burst a bubble of happiness, but I knew I had said what the Lord had prompted me to say.

A few months later I heard that the engagement was off. The wedding had been canceled. I asked a friend of the couple what had happened. This friend said only, "I think it was a case of 'he couldn't give enough' and 'she couldn't get enough.'" And then this friend added, "What's amazing is that I think she knew it. She knew that she didn't love him enough to give in return. She's the one who finally broke off the engagement."

> A good marriage happens when both the wife and the husband are generous givers to each other. Real love means you can't ever seem to give enough. It's not about getting; it's about unselfishly giving.

I was glad she had. She hadn't loved him with a sustaining, giving love.

About two years later, I saw this young woman again, and she said, "Oh, Dr. Stanley, I have the best news! I just got married a couple of months ago and we are so much in love. I found a man that I *want* to give to. I can't get enough of him—his presence, his affection—but I also can't give enough to him. I love thinking of new ways to help him and give to him, and the more I do, the more my love grows for him. Thank you for what you said to me. It kept me from making a huge mistake."

After I shared this story with the man who had come to me for advice, he nodded and said, "You're right. Love is all about giving. I want to give to my wife. I guess I thought if I just gave *more*, she'd love me."

"You can't make another person love you," I said. "You can't make another person stay with you if that person really wants to leave."

"Should I just let her go?"

"No," I said. "Your marriage is worth a fight. Try to talk to her about going to a godly counselor. Try to communicate with her. But in the end, if she is determined to walk out, you have to *give* her the freedom to do that. You may have to love her enough to let her go."

HOW MUCH SHOULD YOU COMPROMISE?

How far are we to compromise to reach peace? The Bible gives a very clear answer. We are to compromise according to the strength, grace, goodness, and love God gives us, all the way to the point where compromising would mean violating a scriptural principle or commandment.

If your compromise means caving in to evil, breaking a commandment related to morality, denying or rebelling against a principle related to godly relationships, turning away from the Bible as the truth of God, or turning away from following Jesus as your Lord, then you must not compromise. You must not violate the Word of God.

Forgive a person seventy times seven? Yes.

Go the second mile, third mile, even the hundredth mile? Yes.

Disobey God's Word—either His commandments or basic principles? No.

Jesus could have achieved peace by compromising with the religious leaders of His day, but to do so would have been to violate the principles of God's love, forgiveness, and grace extended to "whosoever" might believe in His name and be saved. Jesus did not compromise for "peace at any price," and He does not call us to seek peace at any price.

The apostle Paul also could have achieved peace with the religious leaders of his time, and with the Roman Empire for that matter. All He had to state was that Jesus was just a good teacher and that salvation was possible by means other than Jesus' death on the cross. To do that, however, would have been to violate God's truth. Paul did not choose compromise for "peace at any price." Rather, he was willing to be hunted, taunted, banished, and at times physically hurt for his refusal to compromise the truth of God's Word.

> **Jesus did not compromise for "peace at any price," and He does not call us to seek peace at any price.**

You must also never compromise what you believe to be a very direct, specific, clear call of God on your life. If you blatantly and willfully rebel against God's clear call to you, you will find that God will allow you to experience the full consequences of your rebellion, and He will withdraw His hand from your life.

You must also never compromise on the truth of God's Word.

We seem to live in an age in which people hate the idea of absolute truth. They believe in relative truth, saying certain things are "true to *me*" but not necessarily true for all people. They hate God's Word, because God's Word proclaims commandments and truths that apply to all people, of all cultures and nationalities, all races, all ages, and for all generations since the beginning of time.

I recently saw part of a conversation between a television talk-show host and a teenage girl. The host asked her, "Do you believe premarital sex is right or wrong?" She said, "Well, it's not right for *me*, but other people can do what they want. It might be right for *them*." I hear that sentiment expressed over and over by teenagers and others—not just about premarital sex, but about all kinds of behaviors the Bible calls sin.

When it comes to God's Word, the person who believes in relative truth, as compared to absolute truth, tends to say, "Well, that's what *you* believe. That's *your* interpretation."

I assure you of this: If you refuse to compromise your deeply held convictions, the call of God on your life, and the truth of God's Word, then God will stand with you. Furthermore, He will turn any persecution you experience to your eternal benefit. He will bring about spiritual growth, greater faith, and stronger enduring power in you. He will reward you either on earth or in heaven for your stand. And He will give you His peace!

TWELVE

❧

OVERCOMING FEAR

Many people think the opposite of fear is hope, or courage, or strength. The true opposite of fear is *faith*. And when fear causes paralysis, it not only quenches one's peace but it attacks the foundation of that peace—namely, our faith. Peace goes out the window when fear is present. In many polls taken since the 9/11 terrorist attacks, the evidence shows that large segments of our population are living in fear—fear of traveling, of impending doom, of strangers, etc. The other side of the coin is, of course, the majority of these fearful people are not experiencing peace—the calmness of soul, the elimination of anxieties, and the serenity necessary to conduct one's normal affairs in a steady, fear-free manner.

The true opposite of fear is *faith*.

Much of fear is rooted in doubt that God will be present, provide justice or help, or be capable of dealing with the crisis at hand. Faith says, "Yes, God is here. Yes, God will provide. Yes, God is capable of all things!"

Much of fear is rooted in threats—sometimes threatening words, sometimes threatening behavior. Faith says, "I will not be traumatized by threats. I will act wisely, not fearfully. I believe God will prevent whatever the threat is from ever coming to pass. And if the threat does come to pass, I believe God will help me deal with whatever is thrown at me."

When Saul, king of Israel, realized that God had taken His hand of anointing and blessing from him because of his arrogance and disobedience, and had placed it upon the young man David, he was furious. He began a campaign to find David and kill him—to remove this threat from his life. On the other hand, David felt threatened by Saul's army and on several occasions feared for his life, but the Scriptures tell us that David was strengthened by God's promises to protect him and one day make him king of Israel.

In our modern world we often read of people who, in spite of intimidation by disease, accident, or danger, pressed ahead to uncertain outcomes—rejection, defeat, and, yes, sometimes victory. Arctic explorers, Olympic athletes, missionaries, venture capitalists, and philanthropists come to mind. So threats do not have to stymie and cripple us.

Some years ago, I felt threatened by the potential backlash that could occur when I announced that my wife was seeking a divorce. In many churches, for the pastor's marriage to be in trouble is tantamount to his being identified as a moral failure. I had great inner concerns when the announcement was made.

When I told the board of my church, they responded by saying, in essence, "You've been here for us during difficult times. Now we're going to be here for you during this difficult time.

You've been here for us when we needed you, and now we're going to be here for you because you need us."

I felt great encouragement when various board members told me that they knew the kind of man I am. They knew my character and my devotion to the Lord. They knew that I lived what I preached to the best of my ability. They would stand with me regardless of what eventually happened.

Our challenge in times of threat is not to focus on what *might* become a reality, but rather, to focus on what we can count on being true!

Many people are living under a dark cloud of threat today. Some are experiencing the threat of disease, some are facing the threats of injury to their children, and some are hearing threats related to the loss of their job.

The answer to all these types of threat is *faith* in what we *know* to be true about God and about His love and care for us and His ability to provide for all we need—especially His peace, which can help carry us through anything.

THE NATURE OF OUR FEARS

Once when I was about fifteen, I was down at a creek by myself. There was a big rock there that we used to dive off of, and for some reason that day I decided that I'd dive off and then stand on my head in the water. I dived, got myself perfectly balanced in a headstand underwater, and then I couldn't seem to get myself unbalanced. The current kept me in an upright position, my head at the bottom of the creek bed, no matter which way I moved. I panicked, thinking, *I'm going to drown!* Somehow I had the sense to push up and tumble forward and, as quickly as possible, get my head out of the water so I could breathe.

That kind of fear is a normal, natural, instinctual fear associated with physical survival.

Identify your fears. What do you fear most?

Death? Being alone? Old age?

Do you fear being rejected or criticized, or losing someone you love?

Do you fear poor health or perhaps the possibility of developing a particular disease?

Do you fear a tragedy involving a child or spouse?

Fear can sometimes lurk in our hearts in such a subtle way that we don't even identify the feeling we have as fear. It may be that we have a sense of foreboding, an uneasiness, or a feeling of dread.

Let's take a look at several of the biggest and most common fears we all face.

FEAR OF SIN'S CONSEQUENCES

Fear is a normal and universal response to our *knowing* we have sinned and become separated from God. Fear of this type is the first emotion we find in the Bible. In the third chapter of Genesis we read that Adam and Eve heard God walking in the garden in the cool of the day, and they hid themselves from God's presence. God called to them, and Adam replied, "I heard Your voice in the garden, and I was afraid because I was naked; and I hid myself" (Gen. 3:10).

A recognition of our own sin always makes us feel exposed and vulnerable to God's judgment. There is a fear of being "found out" and chastised.

> **Fear is a normal and universal response to our *knowing* we have sinned and become separated from God.**

God actually built the emotion of fear into our human nature so that we might flee danger. His intent was that Adam and Eve flee from the presence of Satan, the serpent who came with temptations in the Garden of Eden. That is the rightful purpose and function of fear—to cause us to turn and walk away from the devil's temptations any and every time they come.

FEAR OF DANGER AND HARM

Since the fall of man in the Garden of Eden, fear was not only to be the emotion a person felt in the presence of Satan, but also the first emotion a person felt in the presence of anything associated with death, destruction, or danger. It is the first emotion we are to feel in the presence of evil of any kind, from any source. In our fear we are to take precautions or adopt a defensive posture in anticipation of an assault or, if possible, flee the scene—commonly known as the fight-or-flight reaction.

So we have a number of natural, normal fears—such as the fear of falling, the fear associated with coming in contact with a burning stove, or the fear of crossing a busy freeway at rush hour. These are fears that help protect us and preserve life. They turn us away from harm and pain and help us avoid injury, not only physically but emotionally and spiritually.

I have a very healthy fear of snakes. I've had that fear since I was in my twenties. I was walking one day with a member of the church where I was the pastor, and suddenly he said, "Stop. Don't take another step." It was early in the morning, and the shadows were crossing the path we were walking. I looked ahead, and there in the shadows I saw what he had already seen. A rattlesnake was coiled as if preparing to strike.

I stood absolutely still, too frightened to even blink or speak in reply, until that snake uncoiled itself and slithered off to the side of the path.

Was that a normal response? Yes, it was. Has that fear of snakes contributed to my being alive today? Very likely. As much time as I have spent in wilderness areas in my life, my fear of snakes no doubt has kept me from harm on a number of occasions. I give snakes plenty of opportunity to get out of my way!

Normal and positive fears are not only related to natural phenomena or creatures. They are also related to internal human attitudes. For example, it should be the norm for a person to fear taking a hallucinogenic drug, to the point where that person refuses to experiment or try that drug. It should be the norm for a young person to fear engaging in sex apart from marriage, not only because of the danger of unwanted pregnancy or contracting a sexually transmitted disease, but also because of the emotional danger of finding oneself feeling rejected, lonely, ashamed, and guilty for disobeying God's commandments. It should be the norm for a person to fear getting into a car that is about to be driven by a person who has been drinking alcohol. It should be the norm for a person to fear the consequences that may come from committing a crime. Fear can be an agent of protection for our physical lives *and* the well-being of our souls.

God never intended, however, that we be afraid of Him or

afraid of our future in Him. When we read in the Bible about having a "fear" of the Lord, that term *fear* actually refers to great reverence, honor, or awe. It is an awe rooted in our awareness that God governs all things and is absolutely righteous in all His judgments. An awesome awareness and reverence of the glory of God produce humility and obedience.

God also never intended that we live in fear that keeps us from seeking a deeper relationship with Him or that keeps us from going about normal daily life or fulfilling the responsibilities we have to others. The apostle Paul wrote to Timothy, his coworker in the ministry, saying, "God has not given us a spirit of fear, but of power and of love and of a sound mind" (2 Tim. 1:7).

Any fear that keeps you from being a witness for the gospel, makes you cower in weakness before other people, keeps you from reaching out in love to those in need, or keeps you from behaving in a rational manner is *not* a normal fear God intends for you to have!

FEAR OF EVIL

Spiritual dangers are just as real as physical dangers. It is *good* for a person to be fearful in evil situations.

Many years ago, I traveled with a group of seventeen people from my church in Ohio to do missions work for two weeks in Haiti. While in Haiti we watched a man performing a dance. As he danced and whirled his machete in our direction, I suddenly felt a horrible presence of evil all around us. Momentarily, I was filled with fear for my physical safety and the safety of the people with me. My immediate response to this fear was anger, and out of that anger I began to pray and intercede for our safety.

This fear was rooted in the *spirit* realm. It was a fear I've come to recognize as a fear that any Christian *should* feel in the face of pure evil.

Why do I say it is a good thing to feel fear of evil? Because that fear can and should drive you to pray, to trust God to deliver you from the power of evil, and to get as far away from evil as possible!

FEAR OF DISOBEYING GOD

It is also good to have a fear of disobeying God. That fear can and *should* compel a person to obey!

One of the times I was most afraid in my life was the time I was first elected president of the Southern Baptist Convention. I felt very inadequate, and I really didn't want the position. It was a time of much division and heartache among the fifteen million or so Southern Baptists, and although some of the leaders of the convention wanted me to run for the office, I told God and these men and women that I did not want to.

The night before the nominations, I was in a meeting with a group of preachers and one missionary woman. This woman boldly said to me, "Charles Stanley, get on your knees and repent. You are God's choice to be president. Get on your knees and repent!" I fell to my knees immediately! I prayed, but I still resisted in my heart.

I told God repeatedly that there were men who were much more qualified for the job. I told Him that there were men better suited in temperament for the position. I reminded the Lord about how much animosity other people in the denomination were feeling toward me. I asked Him to call somebody else.

The morning of the nominations, I awoke with a firm decision in my heart that I wasn't going to allow my name to be put into nomination for the presidency. As I prepared to leave the hotel room, I reached out to put my hand on the doorknob, and God spoke to my heart, *Don't put your hand on that doorknob until you are willing to do what I tell you to do.* I fell to my knees at the end of the bed, sobbing. I knew I had to do this, or I would be in disobedience. I told the Lord once again that I really didn't want to do this, but at the same time, I knew I had to agree to be nominated. I remember thinking, *Maybe the Lord just wants to humble me, and that will be the end of it.*

I went over to the place where a number of pastors and other church leaders were in a prayer meeting. I said to a friend of mine, "I think *you* ought to do this." He said, "I'm not going to do it." The Lord spoke in my heart, *Tell them,* and I heard myself saying, "I'll do it." Immediately, I became gripped with overwhelming fear. I felt as if I were falling off a mountaintop, headed for a crash on the rocks far below. Other people in the room, however, began to pray with great rejoicing. I finally concluded, "Okay, Lord, I'm doing what I believe You have told me to do." And in coming to that conclusion and affirmation, fear left.

After the votes were counted, amazingly to me, I won the election.

No sooner was I elected than a group of men set out to destroy my reputation and keep me from being an effective leader. That didn't bother me. I wasn't afraid of *that.* Once the issue was settled, it was settled for me. I put all my efforts into being the best president I knew how to be, with God's guidance and strength.

I learned in that experience that faith in God is *always* more powerful than fear. I also learned that an ongoing trust in God can keep fear from becoming a dictating, domineering emotion.

REAL OR SHADOW FEARS?

The fears I have described above are normal, and in many ways helpful. They are *real* fears.

Shadow fears, however, are those that are not real. They reside only in our imaginations or our minds. If they persist or grow, they can result in a person's developing a "spirit of fear."

A spirit of fear enslaves a person's mind and heart. The person who has a spirit of fear, which may be anything from a serious phobia to a paralyzing or crippling fear that keeps that person from functioning normally in relationships with other people, is a person who becomes a *slave* to fear. Such a person won't go certain places, engage in certain activities, or speak out in certain situations because he or she fears great loss, injury, persecution, or retribution.

The first goal many of us have when dealing with fear is determining if the fear we feel is legitimate or if it is a shadow fear.

Researchers who have studied fear have concluded that there is virtually no difference in our physiological reaction to these two types of fear. The physiological response made by a person who comes into contact with a live bear is almost identical to the physiological response of a person who sees dimly in the shadows a person who is dressed up to look like a bear.

The same thing holds true for fears rooted in our emotions. Fears related to our feelings of self-worth or self-esteem are especially damaging. For example, the person who fears rejection tends to respond to other people out of that fear whether or not the fear is justified. And the results or consequences are the same, whether or not the assessment is valid!

Some shadow fears come from bad teaching. Fears about whether one will get to heaven often develop because people have been taught incorrectly about God's power to forgive or about God's gift of eternal life. Fears about God happen when people have been taught the wrong things about the true nature of God.

Other shadow fears arise because of prejudices or from the bad influence of parents when we were young children.

Like anxiety, slavish, crippling, paralyzing fear:

- clouds the mind—it stifles thinking and snuffs out creativity.

- causes tension in the body, which often leads to temporary emotional paralysis or a failure to act.

- weakens our confidence and boldness, especially in declaring the goodness of God or the good news about Jesus Christ as Savior.

- keeps us from praying, and especially from praying boldly and with faith.

- keeps us from reaching the full potential that God has for us in every area of our lives.

A fear that constricts or limits us does not *fit* who we are to be as sons and daughters of the almighty God.

The key questions we must ask in determining whether a fear is normal, real, and helpful or if it is debilitating, enslaving, and paralyzing are these: "What does God say about this fear? Does He say that this is something I should fear? Or does He say that He is sufficient in all ways to meet my needs so that I don't need to fear this thing, this relationship, this action, this possibility, or this situation?"

SEVEN STEPS TO OVERCOMING FEAR

There are several steps we can take to overcome fear.

1. ACKNOWLEDGE THE FEAR YOU EXPERIENCE

Acknowledge that you are fearful. Ask God to help you identify the fear—to name it, define it, and bring it to the surface of your conscience so you can talk about it and confess its presence to the Lord.

Don't deny that you feel fear. Don't think that you are too "mature" to be afraid. We never become so spiritually mature that we do not feel fear—either the natural and normal fear that helps in our preservation and protection, or spiritual attacks of fear. Fear can grip any of us.

David, who had experienced the power of God to protect him and preserve his life in numerous situations, still wrote:

> My heart is severely pained within me,
> And the terrors of death have fallen upon me.
> Fearfulness and trembling have come upon me,
> And horror has overwhelmed me.
> So I said, "Oh, that I had wings like a dove!
> I would fly away and be at rest.

Indeed, I would wander far off,

And remain in the wilderness." (Ps. 55:4–7)

> **We never become so spiritually mature that we do not feel fear—either the natural and normal fear that helps in our preservation and protection, or spiritual attacks of fear. Fear can grip any of us.**

Don't just accept a fear in your life as something harmless. The reality is that fear keeps you from going some places God desires you to go. It can keep you from doing some things that God may desire you to do.

Acknowledge your fear. Face up to it.

2. ASK IMMEDIATELY FOR GOD'S HELP

Go to your heavenly Father immediately to ask Him to help you conquer your fear. Ask the Lord to cleanse your mind of fearful thoughts. Ask Him to protect your mind from gripping fear. Ask Him to prepare you to counteract fear in positive, strong ways.

The psalmist wrote:

> I sought the LORD, and He heard me,
> And delivered me from all my fears. (Ps. 34:4)

3. DETERMINE THE ROOT FEAR

Ask God to help you identify any emotions that may be linked to fear, such as:

greed – fear of not having enough

rejection – fear of not being accepted

guilt – fear of being found out

lack of confidence – fear of failure

anger – fear of not getting your own way, losing control or
      esteem

jealousy – fear of not having what you believe is rightfully yours

indecisiveness – fear of criticism, fear of making a wrong
      decision

I recently heard about a woman who was very afraid of going outside after dark, even though she lives in what many would consider to be a very safe neighborhood. She is afraid even to go out to her car in the driveway or to turn off the sprinklers in the yard.

A pastor I know asked her why she thought she had this fear. She didn't know. She said she had always been afraid of the dark. I could relate at that point. As a boy I was very afraid of being alone in the dark.

The pastor probed further, "But *why* do you think you are afraid of the dark?"

She said, "I guess because I think something bad could happen to me in the dark, and I wouldn't see it coming in time to protect myself."

"Do you think you are totally responsible for protecting yourself in the dark?" the pastor asked.

"I never really have thought about that," the woman said.

The pastor went on, "Do you think it is possible that God desires to protect you, His child, when you are alone in the dark?"

"Well, yes," she said, and a tear began to flow down her cheek.

The counselor said, "This woman came to realize that the fear beneath the obvious fear was a fear that God might not always be there for her. We went through about a dozen passages in the Bible that assure us of God's constant presence with those of us who have accepted Jesus as our Savior.

> **Your ability to see Him present with you, just inches away from you and walking with you stride by stride, may very well be the key to your walking in faith, not fear.**

"She finally said to me, 'I'm not afraid of the dark! I'm afraid God is negligent! I've got to start seeing God as standing right by my side *all* the time, and especially in the dark.'"

The truth is, *God is always by your side.*

Your ability to see Him present with you, just inches away from you and walking with you stride by stride, may very well be the key to your walking in faith, not fear.

4. GO TO GOD'S WORD

The Bible has dozens of "fear not" verses. I especially like Isaiah 41:9–13 as a passage of Scripture that confronts fear:

You whom I have taken from the ends of the earth,
And called from its farthest regions,
And said to you,
"You are My servant,

I have chosen you and have not cast you away:

Fear not, for I am with you;

Be not dismayed, for I am your God.

I will strengthen you,

Yes, I will help you,

I will uphold you with My righteous right hand."

Behold, all those who were incensed against you

Shall be ashamed and disgraced;

They shall be as nothing,

And those who strive with you shall perish.

You shall seek them and not find them—

Those who contended with you.

Those who war against you

Shall be as nothing,

As a nonexistent thing.

For I, the LORD your God, will hold your right hand,

Saying to you, "Fear not, I will help you."

Read that entire chapter aloud to yourself—in fact, read it repeat-edly if you need to. Let the words sink deep into your spirit.

Read and memorize verses that deal with fear. Psalm 56 is a wonderful psalm for those who are fearful that their critics or ene-mies will destroy their work, reputation, influence, or property.

Be merciful to me, O God, for man would swallow me up;

Fighting all day he oppresses me.

My enemies would hound me all day,

For there are many who fight against me, O Most High

Whenever I am afraid,

I will trust in You.

In God (I will praise His word),

In God I have put my trust;

I will not fear.

What can flesh do to me?

All day they twist my words;

All their thoughts are against me for evil.

They gather together,

They hide, they mark my steps,

When they lie in wait for my life.

Shall they escape by iniquity?

In anger cast down the peoples, O God!

You number my wanderings;

Put my tears into Your bottle;

Are they not in Your book?

When I cry out to You,

Then my enemies will turn back;

This I know, because God is for me.

In God (I will praise His word),

In the LORD (I will praise His word).

In God I have put my trust;

I will not be afraid.

What can man do to me?

Vows made to You are binding upon me, O God;

I will render praises to You,

For You have delivered my soul from death.

Have You not kept my feet from falling.

That I may walk before God

In the light of the living?

Psalm 91, which I mentioned in an earlier chapter, is a tremendous psalm that addresses feelings of fear:

> He who dwells in the secret place of the Most High
> Shall abide under the shadow of the Almighty.
> I will say of the LORD, "He is my refuge and my fortress;
> My God, in Him I will trust."
> Surely He shall deliver you from the snare of the fowler
> And from the perilous pestilence.
> He shall cover you with His feathers,
> And under His wings you shall take refuge;
> His truth shall be your shield and buckler.
> You shall not be afraid of the terror by night,
> Nor of the arrow that flies by day,
> Nor of the pestilence that walks in darkness,
> Nor of the destruction that lays waste at noonday.
> A thousand may fall at your side,
> And ten thousand at your right hand;
> But it shall not come near you.
> Only with your eyes shall you look,
> And see the reward of the wicked.
> Because you have made the LORD, who is my refuge,
> Even the Most High, your dwelling place,
> No evil shall befall you,
> Nor shall any plague come near your dwelling;
> For He shall give His angels charge over you,
> To keep you in all your ways.
> In their hands they shall bear you up,
> Lest you dash your foot against a stone.

You shall tread upon the lion and the cobra,
The young lion and the serpent you shall trample underfoot.
"Because he has set his love upon Me, therefore I will deliver him;
I will set him on high, because he has known My name.
He shall call upon Me, and I will answer him;
I will be with him in trouble;
I will deliver him and honor him.
With long life I will satisfy him,
And show him My salvation."

Focus on passages in which various individuals in the Bible faced fear. Note the way God dealt with them and how He directed them. For example: Moses felt fear about returning to Egypt (Ex. 3). Esther felt fear in confronting Haman (Est. 3–5).

Memorize verses that speak to God's desire for you to walk in faith. Saturate your mind with passages that build up your faith.

5. PRAISE THE LORD

As you read and speak God's Word, accompany the truth of God's Word with your vocal and frequent praise.

Here are three of my favorite passages to use in confronting fear:

• The LORD is my strength and song,
  And He has become my salvation. (Ps. 118:14)

• The voice of rejoicing and salvation
  Is in the tents of the righteous;
  The right hand of the LORD does valiantly.

The right hand of the LORD is exalted;

The right hand of the LORD does valiantly.

I shall not die, but live,

And declare the works of the LORD. (Ps. 118:15–17)

- I will extol You, my God, O King;

  And I will bless Your name forever and ever.

  Every day I will bless You,

  And I will praise Your name forever and ever.

  Great is the LORD, and greatly to be praised;

  And His greatness is unsearchable. (Ps. 145:1–3)

6. TAKE A POSITIVE STEP

Jesus often asked those He delivered or healed to take a positive action as part of their deliverance or healing. A paralyzed man, for example, was told to pick up his pallet and leave the pool of Bethesda. A blind man was told to go wash in the pool of Siloam.

I believe it is very important for a person to confront fear by taking a positive step in faith. Do something that gives you an experience in which God can reveal to you that He is greater than the fear you have felt.

I recently heard about a woman who had an irrational fear of walking on the grates in the sidewalks of San Francisco. She had a fear that one of them would collapse as she stepped on it and that she would go tumbling into the space below. She asked the Lord to deliver her from this fear, and in her spirit she felt the Lord speaking to her, "Go for a walk with Me." She went out on the street, knowing the Lord wanted her to walk on every grate that she encountered. Seven grates later, she returned to her apartment and again felt in her spirit the Lord speaking to her, "I am walking with you wherever you walk."

Most people know the story of David and Goliath. But one of the important facts of that story that many people overlook is this: David *ran* toward Goliath. He ran in *faith* based upon God's previous deliverance of him from a bear and lion. He ran in *confidence*, knowing God had given him the ability to both run fast and use a sling well. He ran with *wisdom*, knowing he had chosen exactly the right stones.

As you look back over your life, you no doubt can recount many instances in which God has been with you in fearful circumstances. He has delivered you before. He has given you certain abilities and strengths. He promises in His Word to impart wisdom to you if you will only ask. At times you need to confront a frightening situation in a very direct and practical way. Run toward that thing that is causing fear, trusting God even as you go. The words of David are good ones to memorize: "I come to you in the name of the LORD of hosts . . . This day the LORD will deliver you into my hand . . . The battle is the LORD's" (1 Sam. 17:45–47).

7. MAKE A DECISION

Come to a firm decision that you are not going to live in fear. Make a choice to believe God—yes, believe Him more than you believe your own emotions.

You may not get to the point of *complete* faith and trust immediately. The growth of faith takes time and testings, seeing that God is faithful in situation after situation, crisis after crisis, hurtful circumstance after hurtful circumstance. Our faith and confidence in the Lord grow as God reveals His faithfulness to us over time. You can begin, however, to act on your decision to have faith by saying to the Lord every time fear strikes, *God, You are in control of my life, not just some of the time, but all the time.*

Also make a decision that you are not going to be afraid of God. My concept of God as a child was that God was a stern judge sitting up in heaven just waiting for me to make a mistake so He could punish me. I tried hard to please Him, and much of the time as a child I didn't think I did a very good job. I lived in fear that God would place a terrible disease on me or I'd die in a gruesome accident. I imagined something terrible, really bad—the most bloody and awful judgment!

Now when I think about my loving heavenly Father, my thoughts are the exact opposite. I don't see Him as a judge but as my sustainer, protector, provider, and preserver of life. I know that He will forgive me if I sin and that I am eternally secure in my salvation. I know that His desire for me is always something that will lead to my eternal good.

Make a decision that you are going to believe in God, who loves you, provides for you, cares for you, is always available to you, and is in control of your life at all times. Make a decision to trust Him.

As you do, I have no doubt that God can melt away your crippling fears so you can truly experience the depth of His abiding peace.

❦

THIRTEEN

Learning to Live
in Contentment

I awoke one morning at a campsite high in the Canadian
Rockies after nearly two weeks of photography in one of the
most majestic and beautiful areas of the world. With me were
several men from my church. We had enjoyed a time of rich spiritual fellowship as well as a wonderful backcountry adventure. I
was sorry to see the experience come to an end, but I was also
looking forward to getting back to my preaching schedule in
Atlanta.

We spent much of the day breaking camp and traveling to the
city where we were to spend the night before flying home. When
we walked into the hotel, one of the first things the hotel clerk
said to us was, "There's a problem back home."

Immediately we looked at one another in concern. Our minds
raced to our families.

The clerk seemed to read our minds, "Oh, it isn't anything
with your families. Your nation is under attack."

We hurried upstairs and gathered in one of the rooms to
turn on the television set. There on the screen was an image of

a high-rise building on fire, and then the very next image was one of people jumping from the upper floors.

I stared in shock at the news that began to unfold as various reporters recapped the events of the day, September 11, 2001. It took a couple of hours for the whole of the story to sink in. Two airplanes had plowed into the Twin Towers of the World Trade Center, and the towers had subsequently collapsed. Thousands were feared dead. Thousands more had apparently outrun the huge billow of dust and debris and had escaped with minor to severe injuries. A third plane had crashed into the side of the Pentagon and had burst into flames, killing an untold number of people. A fourth plane, which some were already projecting had been heading for the Capitol or the White House, had crashed in a field in Pennsylvania. The vice president and key government leaders had been taken to secure locations as a precaution. The president had just returned to the White House after a series of flights that had taken him to several secure locations in various parts of the United States. Our nation was clearly under attack by terrorists.

About a week later, I found myself standing at Ground Zero. Like many people who stood in that spot, I could scarcely comprehend the magnitude of the devastation before me. It's one thing to see a tragedy that, at best, is a couple of feet high on a television screen. It's another to stand in front of ten stories' worth of twisted metal and concrete, with smoke still rising from mountains of smoldering debris.

I felt a wave of emotions:

- sadness and grief

- anger

- despair

- helplessness

- emptiness

- loneliness

- uncertainty

I also had a general feeling of "pressure" that I could not identify—perhaps sorrow, perhaps shock, perhaps a knowing that life in our nation had been changed in ways we had yet to realize.

As I listened to the firemen, volunteers, and family members of the victims and the survivors tell their stories, I heard still more emotions being voiced:

- confusion

- fear and concerns for safety

- regret at not saying a final good-bye, asking for forgiveness, or having an opportunity to say "I love you"

- honor and pride at the work of the brave rescue workers

- discouragement at the enormity of the task that lay ahead

- doubt that life would ever again have moments of joy

In the days following that trip, I, like many people, had trouble concentrating or focusing on certain tasks. I felt that I had very low supplies of energy and creativity. I longed to escape the reality of what had happened and return to what seemed like the simpler, more secure, and less vulnerable life we had all known just weeks before. I longed for contentment—a return to experiencing an abiding peace. I realized that, as a nation, we were going to have to relearn how to be content and how to feel contentment.

A fact that many people don't recognize is that learning to live in a state of contentment is a growing, maturing, learning process. Taking steps to regain our peace in the aftermath of tragedy is part of the learning process.

An Example of "Learned Contentment"

Earlier in this book, I described the aged apostle Paul's situation—jailed, chained to guards, and yet able to write to the church in Philippi. He chose to write about the importance of their being filled with joy and not anxiety, of their praying in all things—yes, even in their troubled times—with faith in God's powerful presence to protect them. He wrote about how they should live with the peace of God filling their hearts and minds. It was quite a letter to his fellow believers!

There is nothing in his letter that even hints at his being troubled in spirit by his circumstance. There is no hint of anger, which could have been expected, since he was imprisoned unjustly. There is no hint of frustration at his not being able to get out and preach freely as he once had preached. There is no hint of fear, even though his life was in imminent danger. Rather, his letter is filled with contentment, joy, and *peace*.

Sixteen times in just this one letter Paul refers to the "joy of the Lord." And then, as if to top off all that he had said about joy in the midst of suffering, he says,

> I have learned in whatever state I am, to be content: I know how to be abased, and I know how to abound. Everywhere and in all things I have learned both to be full and to be hungry, both to abound and to suffer need. I can do all things through Christ who strengthens me. (Phil. 4:11–13)

The apostle Paul had to *learn* to be content. In admitting that to the Philippians, he was admitting that he hadn't always been content. He had undergone a learning process to get to the point where he could say, "I have learned in whatever state I am, to be content" (Phil. 4:11).

Paul faced both internal and external struggles in his life. These struggles were ones that would have ruffled or shattered even the greatest degree of peace ever felt by any person.

An External Struggle

In his traveling and preaching of the gospel, Paul experienced great difficulties. He listed them in a letter to the church at Corinth (2 Cor. 11:23–29):

- Five times he received thirty-nine lashes at the hands of the Jews.

- Three times he was beaten with rods.

- Once he was stoned.

- Three times he was shipwrecked, and one of those times he was in the water for a full night and day.

- "Often" he was in perils of robbers, dangers initiated by his countrymen, and dangers initiated by Gentiles.

- "Often" he faced dangers in his travels, including rough seas that threatened to capsize the ship in which he was sailing.

- "Frequently" he was in prison.

- "Frequently" he faced the possibility of death.

- He knew what it meant to go without sleep, to be hungry, thirsty, cold, and without sufficient clothing on countless occasions.

- He knew what it meant to be criticized, falsely accused, misquoted, misunderstood, and rejected.

AN INTERNAL STRUGGLE

Paul wrote to the Romans about internal struggles he faced: He admitted that often what he wanted to do, he didn't; and those things he wanted to avoid doing, he sometimes did. He, however, found that in Christ there was a solution—namely, the yielding of our lives totally to Him and the ensuing powerful ministry of God's Spirit in us to help us on our way.

It is as we become conscious moment by moment that Christ is living out His life in us by the presence of God's Spirit, that we have a greater and greater desire to obey Him, and to run to Him quickly for forgiveness any time we become aware that we have disobeyed Him. The more we obey the Lord, the easier we find it is to trust Him. The more we trust Him, the greater peace we feel.

Paul learned to be content in all these diverse and difficult circumstances—external and internal struggles, by learning to trust God. That's right—learning to trust God. We learn contentment through learning to trust Him.

> **The more we obey the Lord, the easier we find it is to trust Him. The more we trust Him, the greater peace we feel.**

And one of the greatest lessons that you can learn as you learn to live in contentment is this: You have the power to *respond* to any situation, not merely react to it. The power of the Holy Spirit resident in you will always enable you to confront a problem with faith and wisdom if you will only trust Him.

FOUR KEYS TO LIVING IN CONTENTMENT

To live in a lasting, confident state of inner contentment, there are several things we must do. First, a word to those of you who are in a relationship with someone that seems to bring you discontentment, rather than peace and satisfaction. You may be living in a situation where one party is unwilling to give you unconditional love or friendship. In other words, from your perspective, there always seems to be an "If" before the promise—"If you do this, we can . . ." or "If you agree, then perhaps . . ." In this kind of relationship you need to apply Key #1:

KEY #1: CUT THE "CONDITIONAL" BONDS

Recognize that there is nothing you can do to make another person love you unconditionally. He or she either does or doesn't. There's no earning unconditional love. There's no amount of striving that wins unconditional love. There are no formulas or prescriptions that ensure the unconditional love of another person. In fact, the very words *earn* and *strive* are ones that apply if love is *conditional*!

It takes a long time to get over being in a relationship with a person who gives conditional love, especially if that person is a parent or a spouse.

A person who has lived for years with someone who loved him or her conditionally nearly always is suspicious of the phrase "I love you." In one way or another, that person tends to ask, "Why?" He or she wants to know what the other person is expecting, why the individual is saying "I love you," and what it is that the person wants in order for that loving feeling to be sustained.

The phrase "I love you" may evoke a response of "Well, I must have done something *right;* let me figure out what it was, so I can continue to do that." At times, the response may be, "Uh-oh. I'm probably on the verge of hearing a 'but' on the end of that phrase"—in other words, "I love you, *but* . . ."

The person who is accustomed to conditional love is a person who can never fully relax in a relationship. There's always the potential for making a mistake, missing a cue, or disappointing someone in some way.

The result is tension and an abiding anxiety. In other words, a lack of peace.

The other side of this coin is that it is very difficult to be in a relationship with a person who has never felt unconditional love, doesn't know how to express love, doesn't know how to receive love, and doesn't even know that he doesn't know these basics for a deep friendship or marriage!

When you are free from the bonds of striving to be perfect in another person's eyes, you are then in a position to actively pursue becoming "whole" in God's eyes. For years, one of my friends heard his family say, "A hundred percent is not good enough for our family; you have to earn 110 percent." What a burden for a child to bear as he grew up!

When these false and damaging expectations are recognized for what they are, however, then they can be rejected or modified. The result? No longer is another person setting the standard of perfection in life. Rather, an individual can seek to understand God's ways and perspectives on life—they are not weighty or burdensome. For the Scriptures say, "My yoke is easy and My burden is light."

Turn to God for unconditional love. All of us need to open our hearts to God's unconditional love. No one will ever be able to contain all the love that is flowing from God toward us. But we each can open up more of our hearts to receive more of His love.

How? Explore what God's Word says about His love. As you read a passage of Scripture about God's love, say to the Lord, *I know You love me just that way. Help me never to forget that. Help me to live in that truth.*

Ask the Lord to help you experience His love in a new way. Be still before the Lord. Open your heart to Him. Ask Him to speak to you and to let you feel His close presence. In this way, we will learn contentment and the result will be our hearts at peace.

Seek friends who love unconditionally. Another thing we can do when we are caught up in the vise of trying to earn conditional love is to seek out people who know how to love unconditionally. I'm not at all encouraging a spouse to turn to a person of the opposite sex for love, affection, or a sexual relationship. But rather, I am encouraging deep, abiding, and godly *friendships* with mentors and peers of the same sex who can provide unconditional love.

Seek out people who accept you for who you are as a brother or sister in Christ Jesus, and who seek to help you become all that God created you to be, but who do not pressure you to "perform" in order for them to continue to be your friend. Seek out people in whom you can confide your mistakes and failures, and who will not criticize you for them, but will help you to see that God's desire is for you to live at an even higher level of moral excellence and godly character.

You may find only one such friend or mentor. That's enough. You are truly fortunate if you can develop a small circle of such friends.

Above all, choose to give unconditional love in return. Stick with that friend through thick and thin. Allow that person to fully share his or her thoughts and feelings with you, without judgment. It is as we love in this way that we *are* loved in return.

KEY #2: CAST ALL YOUR CARES ON THE LORD

Beyond receiving the unconditional love of God and others, to live in abiding contentment you must continually cast *all* your cares on the Lord.

The Bible tells us to cast all our cares upon God, for He cares for us (1 Peter 5:7). How do we "cast our care on the Lord"?

Pray. First, we acknowledge to Him our anxiety and our need for peace. Confess any sin that you believe may be associated with your anxiety. Say to the Lord, "I need Your help. I need Your presence and Your comfort and Your provision." Our first response when anxiety hits should be to look heavenward and cry, "Father!"

Jesus went frequently to the Father in prayer. We read in the Gospel accounts how Jesus left His disciples to be alone with God, often praying early in the morning before dawn (Mark 1:35).

Prayer shifts your focus away from the problem and to the One who can give you the answer, solution, or next step to take. Prayer takes your focus off yourself—and your pain and confusion—to the Father, who knows all, controls all, has all power, and is all-loving.

I find it most interesting that we are urged to make our requests known to God. We are to come boldly before our heavenly Father with our specific requests. The Scriptures encourage us, "Let us therefore come boldly to the throne of grace, that we may obtain mercy and find grace to help in time of need" (Heb. 4:16). The Bible further teaches us, "This is the confidence that we have in Him, that if we ask anything according to His will, He hears us. And if we know that He hears us, whatever we ask, we know that we have the petitions that we have asked of Him" (1 John 5:14–15).

Also, we are urged to offer our prayers with thanksgiving. "Thanksgiving" moves our minds from our problems to the One who can solve our problems. When we voice our thanksgiving, our own ears and mind hear what we are saying about God's ability to provide, protect, and preserve—and our faith comes alive.

You are connected in your spirit to the One who has all

answers, all solutions, all provision, all blessings. Your mind is re-focused on the God who saves, delivers, heals, redeems, restores, and multiplies.

With thanksgiving and praise comes deep assurance, and that, in turn, creates peace in our hearts.

> **You are connected in your spirit to the One who has all answers, all solutions, all provision, all blessings.**

Thank God that He is the One who gives us peace, has all power to resolve our problems, all wisdom to know what's best for us, all mercy to forgive, all love to produce what is best for us, and all desire to defeat the enemy, who is attempting to steal from us, destroy us, and kill us.

Praise God for who He is—He is our Savior, Redeemer, Victor, Healer, Deliverer, Counselor, and many other attributes found from cover to cover in the Bible.

There is no substitute for the importance of thanksgiving and praise to living in deep inner contentment.

Give thanks to the Lord daily—and often throughout a day—for all He has done and is doing for you *right now*.

Praise the Lord for who He is in your life *right now*.

Offer thanksgiving and praise with faith. Our petitions, thanksgiving, and praise must all be bathed by our faith. We must truly believe that God is capable and is in control of all things. We must truly believe that God desires our eternal good. We must truly believe that God is our help in time of need.

When we catch even a glimpse of who God is, what God is

capable of doing, and how He desires to exert the full extent of His power, presence, and provision to help us, we can't help but feel faith and hope welling up in us to produce an abiding peace.

Years ago, I went to a hospital waiting room to sit for a while with a woman who was a member of the church I pastored. Her husband was undergoing a serious operation. She told me that she was trusting the Lord, and then she requested that we pray together. I suggested that she start the prayer, and I would finish it. She began to pray, and the longer she prayed, the louder and more frantic she became in her prayer. Very quickly, she was speaking in great anguish and desperation.

As I knelt there by the chair next to her, I thought, *This is not a prayer of faith. This is a prayer filled with fear.* Her total focus was on her husband and the operation—none of her focus was truly on God as the Great Physician, God as the Healer, God as the Restorer, or God who had all things in His sovereign care. I spoke to this woman in the waiting room of the hospital as we were kneeling and praying—in fact I interrupted her prayer and said, "Ma'am. We need to focus on what God can do in that operating room. We need to focus on who He is and what He is capable of doing."

She stopped short. I think she initially was startled that I interrupted her while she was praying, but the truth is, the road she was going down was not a road I could travel in agreement with her.

I began to pray, and she began to weep. I praised God for His great love of her husband and of her, of His absolute authority over everything in that hospital, of His wisdom that could manifest itself in every move the surgeon made, of His tender care of her and all members of her family through the years, and when I said "amen," I saw in her eyes the peace of God, rather than the sheer panic that had been there just minutes before.

I said to her, "Now, let's talk about God. Let's talk about who God is. Let's talk about how God has provided for you and your husband, and how God has protected you and your husband all through your lives. Let's talk about the Lord, who is our Savior. Let's talk about the Holy Spirit, who fills us and guides our every step."

The more we talked about Jesus, the more her peace grew.

I believe the same for you. The more you focus your mind on Jesus and talk about Jesus, the more your peace will grow.

Whatever we ask of God . . .

Whatever we voice in thanksgiving to God . . .

Whatever we declare to be the attributes of God . . .

We must offer with *faith*.

We must truly believe that when we ask of God, He answers.

We must truly believe that He is worthy of all our thanksgiving and praise.

We must truly believe that He is totally capable of handling all things according to the fullness of His plan and purpose for our life.

Ask according to God's will—which is made clear to us in His Word. Any promise, provision, or principle of the Scriptures is for us today just as much as it was for people in Bible times.

Ask with bold confidence because of your relationship with Christ Jesus.

Ask with faith that God hears and answers all prayers for our eternal good and according to His purposes (James 1:6–7).

Ask with expectancy that God will always answer you in an exceedingly loving, direct, and timely manner.

KEY #3: STAY IN THE WORD

In going through difficult times in my life, one of the great blessings of God to me has been the fact that as a pastor I've had the responsibility for preaching regularly, and that, in turn, has required me to stay in the Word. There's no substitute for being in the Word daily—reading it as nourishment for your soul just as regularly as you take in food for your body. Your Bible is the number-one way God speaks to you in a daily way. It is His message to you—His directives, His opinions, His advice, His words of love and comfort, His faith-building admonitions, and His commands.

> **There's no substitute for being in the Word daily—reading it as nourishment for your soul just as regularly as you take in food for your body.**

Trust me on this—the Lord has a way of speaking to you as you read and meditate on the Scriptures so that you will know it is the Lord who is speaking.

When a crisis strikes, remember the promises found in His Word. If you don't know what those promises are, start today to read your Bible and underline or highlight verses, or make a list of verses in the back of your Bible so that in any crisis, you can turn quickly to God's promises. It is his desire to be present with you, provide for you, preserve and protect you, and turn all things to your good.

Memorize the Word of God, especially those passages that speak special comfort and hope to your heart. Don't wait for a crisis to hit. Have a storage bank of Bible verses lodged in your memory so that when a crisis strikes, the Holy Spirit can move your mind immediately to God's Word even if you don't have a Bible with you.

Say to the Lord, "You said . . ." and conclude as you recite each verse, "I know You are always true to Your Word. I am trusting You to faithfully fulfill Your Word to me now."

Recite Scriptures you've memorized. God's Word says that "faith comes by hearing, and hearing by the word of God" (Rom. 10:17). I firmly believe that the degree to which you know the Word of God is directly related to your ability to sustain faith, hope, and peace in a troubling time.

In His teaching and preaching, and especially in His direct dealings with the devil, who came to Him to tempt Him, Jesus used the Word of God. He frequently prefaced His remarks by saying, "It is written." He reminded His followers frequently about the truth of the Scriptures, saying such things as, "Have you not heard of old?" or, "Have you not read?" (Matt. 4).

Recite the Word of God periodically throughout the day to reinforce God's truth to your life—the truth about who He is, who we are, the relationship He desires to have with us, and the relationships He desires for us to have with others.

KEY #4: TAKE CHARGE OF YOUR THINKING

You can control what you think. You and you alone have the ability and the responsibility for *choosing* what you will focus your thoughts upon.

If you need to get up and walk into a different room where you can speak aloud to God and get away from the immediate emotional turmoil of others—then get up and go.

If you need to say to the person on the other end of the line, "I'm going to call you back in a few minutes. Right now, I need to pray about this," then say this, hang up, pray, and get a grip on your thinking so that when you return the call, you can speak with faith.

If you need to turn off negative signals all around you—the horror movie on television, the loud music, the distracting noises—then do so.

So many people just *react* to what is happening around them. Reactions usually begin in our emotions, and the result is that our thoughts become bound up in our emotions, most of which are negative emotions of fear and doubt in a time of severe crisis. Other people react to highly negative circumstances by becoming paralyzed by confusion, tension, and inner turmoil. None of these reactions are what God desires for us!

God calls us to *respond* to life, not merely react to it. Certainly we may react in the initial moment or two of a negative circumstance or crisis. But very quickly, we must speak to our minds, *Don't panic. God is in control!* If you have gone immediately to the Father and cried out to Him for help, adding your proclamations of thanksgiving and praise, and you have done this with faith, then immediately you must follow that time of prayer, praise, and thanksgiving by saying to your mind and heart, *Believe! Trust!*

God calls us to *respond* to life, not merely react to it.

There may be times when you find that you must *force* yourself to think about the goodness of God. Focus on His unconditional love for you and anybody else who may be involved in the crisis you face. Focus on His power and ability to control all circumstances. Focus on His always-listening ear that hears you and His always-watchful eye that sees you day and night.

Remember this: The larger your thoughts about God, the smaller your thoughts about your problem!

Refuse to have a pity party or slide into depression. Choose instead to see God's loving arms wrapped around you, lifting you up to safety, provision, and peace!

MAINTAIN YOUR FOCUS ON THE LORD

All that I have said above points toward this central truth: To live in inner contentment, the entire focus of your life must be the Lord Jesus Christ.

I've had short periods in my life when a particular problem or situation would cause me to have nights in which I'd toss and turn hour after hour, unable to sleep. I have discovered that the best thing I can do when I can't seem to let go of thinking about a particular problem, conversation, or criticism, is to get out of bed, get down on my knees, and cry out to God, "Please help me through this. Help me to focus on You and You alone."

Sleep comes when my focus is on the Lord and on how He would have me think or respond in my emotions to a particular situation. Sleep is elusive when I allow my focus to get on what others have said, all the things that might happen, or the difficulty of a challenge that lies ahead. The choice is really very simple— think about the Lord and His abundant provision, protection, and love, or think about all the people and circumstances that are trying to rob you of provision, destroy your life, or heap hatred upon you.

Thinking about the Lord brings a person peace. Thinking about anything else is usually a shortcut to anxiety, fear, or worry.

It is important when you focus on the Lord that you see the Lord as being in your situation with you, right at that moment. Too many people think of God as being far away—off in heaven somewhere. Others think of God as being in their distant future— when they are older or on the brink of dying. They don't see God as being accessible or available to them in the immediacy of their lives. The truth is, He is present with us in every moment of every day.

See the Lord walking with you in peace. The most peaceful place I have ever been is the Sea of Galilee. Years ago I was at a spot by the sea that seemed to me the very definition of peace and tranquillity.

In today's world, most people probably wouldn't think of that area as being peaceful. It's only a matter of a few dozen miles to Syria and Lebanon from there. People tend to think of Israel as a whole as a hot spot in the world, a place of virtually no peace.

But I felt great peace there. Why? Because I felt the Lord there. I sensed His presence. I was aware of His awesome power and authority over my life.

It is very easy for me to close my eyes and see the Lord walking right beside me along the Sea of Galilee. I also find it very easy and beneficial to envision the Lord walking right beside me in any number of beautiful natural settings I've experienced in the United States and in other nations.

I enjoy walking along an ocean beach, listening to the rhythm of the waves and feeling the sand under my feet.

I enjoy flying in a small plane as the only passenger. As the plane leaves the earth, I am able to shut out the noise of the engines and relax and feel at perfect peace—without concerns, without work, without responsibilities, without pressure, without ringing phones.

I especially enjoy hiking or riding on horseback in the mountains. The quiet and solitude of being high in the mountains is very special to me. There's nothing man-made in sight, no pollution, no noise—just an amazing calm. At night, the stars are so close you could stir them with a spoon.

It's not these *environments* that give peace. It's the awareness of God that I feel in my heart when I am in these environments that produces peace. When I am up high in the mountains, perhaps in a small meadow or by a high-mountain lake, surrounded by peaks, walking about all alone, I have a strong sense of, "Only You know where I am, God. But You know. You know me. You know where I am. And I know You."

It's that sense of "God with me" that is important for me to recapture, to envision, to see with spiritual eyes, when times of trouble hit my life.

Live a Christ-centered life. A self-centered person is a person who thinks, *My needs, my desires, my wants, and my ideas must be met, enacted, and fulfilled.* Such a person tends to talk nonstop about "my career, my accomplishments, my awards, my car, my house, my clothes, my vacation, my pleasure, my, my, my, my." The best three friends of a self-centered person are Me, Myself, and I. Such a person nearly always is very insensitive to others and a manipulator of people and situations. He thinks the world truly *should* revolve around him.

The opposite of being self-centered is to be Christ-centered. It is to say, "What Christ wants is what I want. What pleases Christ is what I desire."

The very same is true, my friend, for your relationship with Christ Jesus. You are going to have to lay aside your personal ambitions and desires, time, material and financial resources, and energy to enter into a deep relationship with Christ Jesus. If you truly are to have fellowship with Him, you'll have a desire to open up and *give* of yourself—truly, give of all aspects of yourself.

Jesus said, "Give, and it will be given to you: good measure, pressed down, shaken together, and running over will be put into your bosom. For with the same measure that you use, it will be measured back to you" (Luke 6:38). Often we think of that verse as referring only to money and material possessions. Jesus meant far more. He meant the giving of your *self* and everything that is within your power of giving. He meant the giving of time, the giving of talent, the giving of resources, the giving of encouraging words, the giving of your presence, and the giving of prayers. He meant all that you might give to Him or give in His name to others.

What a glorious promise is contained in what Jesus said about giving. When you give, you will receive back "good measure, pressed down, shaken together, and running over." What you receive will be in overflowing amounts. The degree of your generosity in giving will be what determines the degree of your abundance in receiving.

Show me a person who is overflowing in generous friendship to another person, and I'll show you a person rich in friendships.

Show me a person who is extremely generous in the giving of her time to other people, and I'll show you a person who always has people "there" for her in times of her need.

Show me a person who can't give enough of himself to further the specific ministry calling that God has placed on his life, and I'll show you a person who has a tremendous sense of purpose and fulfillment.

The person who does not give is a person who does not receive. Such a person cannot experience peace.

Friend, Jesus is the source of your contentment. When you by faith enter into a personal relationship with Jesus you will experience peace.

About the Author

DR. CHARLES F. STANLEY is pastor of the 15,000-member First Baptist Church in Atlanta, Georgia, and is president and CEO of In Touch® Ministries. He has twice been elected president of the Southern Baptist Convention and is well-known internationally through his IN TOUCH radio and television ministry. His many bestselling books include *Walking Wisely*, *When Tragedy Strikes*, *Charles Stanley's Handbook for Christian Living*, *A Touch of His Power*, *Our Unmet Needs*, *Enter His Gates*, and *The Source of My Strength*.

Other Books by Charles Stanley Published by Thomas Nelson Publishers

Charles Stanley's Handbook of Christian Living
Discover Your Destiny
Enter His Gates
Eternal Security
The Gift of Forgiveness
The Gift of Love
The Glorious Journey
How to Handle Adversity
How to Keep Your Kids on Your Team
How to Listen to God
In Touch with God
Into His Presence
Our Unmet Needs
On Holy Ground
The Power of the Cross
Seeking His Face
The Source of My Strength
Success God's Way
Winning the War Within
The Wonderful Spirit-Filled Life

The In Touch Study Series

Advancing Through Adversity
Becoming Emotionally Whole
Developing a Servant's Heart
Developing Inner Strength
Discovering Your Identity in Christ
Experiencing Forgiveness
Experiencing Success God's Way
Exploring the Depths of God's Love
Feeling Secure in a Troubled World
Leaving a Godly Legacy
Listening to God
Living in His Sufficiency
Ministering Through Spiritual Gifts
Overcoming the Enemy
Practicing Basic Spiritual Disciplines
Preparing For Christ's Return
Protecting Your Family
Pursuing a Deeper Faith
Relying on the Holy Spirit
Sharing the Gift of Encouragement
Talking with God
Understanding Eternal Security
Understanding Financial Stewardship
Winning on the Inside

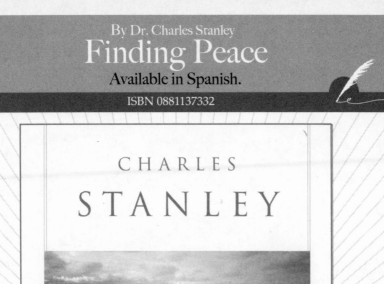